Knowledge and Innovation for Development

This book is dedicated to *Geoffrey Oldham* and *Alberto Giesecke Matto*,
long-term friends and mentors,
and to the memory of
Eric Trist, Jorge Sábato, Máximo Halty, Amílcar Herrera,
Miguel Wionczek and *Marcel Roche*
from whom I learned so much.

Knowledge and Innovation for Development

The Sisyphus Challenge of the 21st Century

Francisco Sagasti

Director, Agenda: PERÚ, Lima, Peru and Visiting Professor at the University for Peace, Costa Rica

Edward Elgar
Cheltenham, UK • Northampton, MA, USA

Published by
Edward Elgar Publishing Limited
Glensanda House
Montpellier Parade
Cheltenham
Glos GL50 1UA
UK

Edward Elgar Publishing, Inc.
136 West Street
Suite 202
Northampton
Massachusetts 01060
USA

A catalogue record for this book
is available from the British Library

Library of Congress Cataloguing in Publication Data

Sagasti, Francisco R.
    Knowledge and innovation for development: the Sisyphus challenge
of the 21st century/Francisco Sagasti.
        p.   cm.
    Includes bibliographical references and index.
    1. Science and state—Developing countries. 2. Technology and
state—Developing countries. 3. Research—Developing countries.
I. Title.
Q127.2.S33   2004
338.9'26'091724—dc22

                                                            2003064253

ISBN 1 84376 653 1 (cased)

Typeset by Manton Typesetters, Louth, Lincolnshire, UK.
Printed and bound in Great Britain by MPG Books Ltd, Bodmin, Cornwall.

Contents

Figures

Tables

Boxes

Abbreviations

ACAST	Advisory Committee on Science and Technology, United Nations
ACSTD	Advisory Committee on Science and Technology for Development, United Nations
BID/IDB	Banco Interamericano de Desarrollo/Inter-American Development Bank
CEPALC/ECLAC	Comisión Económica para América Latina y el Caribe/ Economic Commission for Latin America and the Caribbean, United Nations
CGS	Center for Global Studies, University of Victoria, Victoria, Canada
CIP	Competitive Industrial Performance index
EEA	European Economic Area
EFTA	European Free Trade Agreement
EPO	European Patent Office
EU	European Union
GAVI	Global Alliance for Vaccines and Immunization
GDP	gross domestic product
GEF	Global Environment Facility
GNP	gross national product
GPG	global public goods
GRADE	Grupo de Análisis para el Desarrollo, Lima, Peru
HDI	Human Development Index
HDR	Human Development Report, United Nations Development Programme
HIV/AIDS	Human Immunodeficiency Virus/Acquired Immunodeficiency Syndrome
ICT	information and communications technologies
IDRC	International Development Research Centre, Canada
IDS	Institute of Development Studies at the University of Sussex, UK
IFDA	International Foundation for Development Alternatives, Nyon, Switzerland
INTAL	Instituto para la Integración de América Latina, Buenos Aires, Argentina

IPRs	intellectual property rights
LSMS	Living Standard Measurement Survey
MIT	Massachusetts Institute of Technology
MNE	multinational enterprises
MVA	manufacturing value added
OAS	Organization of American States
OECD	Organization for Economic Cooperation and Development
PPP	purchasing power parity
QEH	Queen Elizabeth House, Oxford University
R&D	research and development
RAWOO	Development Research Assistance Council of the Netherlands
S&T	science and technology
SAREC	Swedish Agency for Research Cooperation
STPI	Science and Technology Policy Instruments
TAI	Technology Achievement Index
TCDC	technical cooperation between developing countries
TRIPS	trade-related aspects of intellectual property rights
UK	United Kingdom
UN	United Nations
UNCSTD	United Nations Conference on Science and Technology for Development
UNCTAD	United Nations Conference on Trade and Development
UNDP	United Nations Development Programme
UNEP	United Nations Environment Programme
UNESCO	United Nations Educational, Scientific and Cultural Organization
UNFSSTD	United Nations Financing System for Science and Technology for Development
UNICEF	United Nations Children's Fund
UNIDO	United Nations Industrial Development Organization
US	United States
USPTO	United States Patent and Trademark Office
WHO	World Health Organization
WWW	World Wide Web

Preface

The first ideas for this book were developed in the late 1960s and early 1970s, as part of my doctoral dissertation in Operations Research and Social Systems Science at the University of Pennsylvania, which was prepared under the direction of professors Russell Ackoff and Eric Trist. The creation of the National Research Council in Peru and the encouragement of Alberto Giesecke Matto, its first President, provided the initial motivation for the research that led to the dissertation. That work was supported by the Technological Development Unit of the Organization of American States, directed by Máximo Halty Carrère, and carried out at the Secretariat of the Andean Common Market and at the Peruvian Ministry of Industry. My ideas evolved in discussions with Jorge Sábato, Miguel Wionczek, Amílcar Herrera, Marcel Roche, Víctor Urquidi, Mauricio Guerrero, Pedroleón Díaz, Alejandro Moya, Carlos Martínez Vidal, Isaías Flit, Gustavo Flores, Gastón Oxman, Luis Soto Krebs and Constantino Vaitsos. The first of my papers on the subject was published in a volume edited by Eugene and Victor Rabinowitch in 1972.

My subsequent involvement in the Science and Technology Policy Instruments (STPI) project provided a rich source of material, ideas, experiences and case studies, as well as intense interactions with dozens of researchers and policy-makers from many developing countries. An intense period of work with Alberto Aráoz, Carlos Contreras, Onelia Cardettini, Alejandro Nadal, Eduardo Amadeo, Luis Stuhlman, Fernando Chaparro, Fabio Erber, Jose Tavares, Ignacio Ávalos, Dulce de Uzcátegui, Yolanda Fombona, KunMo Chung, DukNon Yoon, ChanMo Park, Anil Malhotra, Nikola Kljusev, Adel Sabet, Fernando Gonzáles Vigil, Roberto Wangeman, Genevieve Dean and other members of the STPI national teams and the Field Coordinator's Office, gave me a unique opportunity to see first hand the science and technology policy problems faced by a wide variety of developing countries. The STPI project was primarily supported by the science and technology policy research program of the Canadian International Development Research Centre (IDRC), directed by Geoffrey Oldham whose continuous and generous support over several decades is most gratefully acknowledged. The dissemination of the results of this project, which were undertaken in the late 1970s, provided additional occasions to write and reflect on the problems of science and technology for development. A period of work for the Secretariat of the

1979 United Nations Conference on Science and Technology for Development provided an opportunity to write the position paper of the Secretariat
under the supervision of Guy Gresford. In parallel, an involvement with the
International Foundation for Development Alternatives (IFDA), headed by
Marc Nerfin, helped to sharpen my views on the importance of non-Western
knowledge and technology, and also provided an opportunity to learn from
professor Ignacy Sachs. Other persons that helped to shape my ideas during
this period include Jim Mullin, Louis Berlinguet, Ruth Zagorin, Charles
Weiss, Princeton Lyman, Martin Lees, Lennart Båge, Jurg Mahner, Tony
Tillet, Anna Jaguaribe and Amilcar Ferrari.

During the 1980s I continued to work on science and technology issues
at GRADE, a Peruvian think tank with which I was involved for several
years. With support from the IDRC, from the Swedish Agency for Research
Cooperation (SAREC), and from other international cooperation agencies
and foundations, a number of research projects on science, technology and
development were carried out during this period. At the same time, I became
a member of the Board of the Peruvian National Council for Science and
Technology, a consultant to several national and international organizations
dealing with science and technology for development, and also member (later
Chairman) of the United Nations Advisory Committee on Science and Technology for Development. An assignment as chairman of the evaluation team
for the International Foundation for Science, work with the United Nations
Industrial Development Organization (UNIDO) on market structure and technological behavior, and an involvement with two panels of the United States
National Academy of Sciences provided additional opportunities to broaden
my perspective on these issues.

Work on science, technology and development continued intermittently
during my tenure as Chief of the Strategic Planning Division and Senior
Advisor at the World Bank in the late 1980s and early 1990s, I had the
opportunity to interact with and learn from Carl Dahlman, Colin Bradford,
John Stremlau, Sven Arrhenius, David Hopper and Alexander Shakow, among
other World Bank colleagues. During this period I became a member of the
Task Force on Science and Technology for Development of the Carnegie
Commission on Science and Technology (co-chaired by Rodney Nichols and
Jimmy Carter). A project sponsored by the United Nations University, coor-
dinated jointly with Jean-Jacques Salomon and Cèline Sachs-Jeantet provided
an opportunity to work with a select number of high-level experts in the
preparation of a textbook on science and technology for development.

Upon my return to Peru in 1993, research on the role of knowledge in
development continued with support of the Carnegie Corporation of New
York, headed by David Hamburg and whose science and development program was directed first by Patricia Rosenfield and subsequently by Akin

Adubifa. Work as advisor to the President of the Canadian International Development Research Centre, Keith Bezanson, provided a unique opportunity to interact with him and to appreciate the practical problems of an agency dedicated to building science and technology capacities in developing countries.

An involvement with the World Bank team in charge of the 1998 World Development Report, and with the United Nations Development Programme (UNDP) team in charge of the 2001 Human Development Report, both of which dealt with science and technology for development, provided intellectual stimulus and the opportunity to interact with colleagues interested in the same issues. A decade of work with Agenda: PERÚ in the design of a development strategy for the country through a highly participatory process, helped to place science and technology issues in perspective, linking them to urgent development needs. My work in Agenda: PERÚ also allowed me the opportunity to learn from Max Hernández.

Finally, the opportunity for preparing this book was provided by a grant from the Rockefeller Foundation's program on Global Inclusion, directed by Janet Maughan, which involved joint work with the Center for Global Studies (CGS) at the University of Victoria, Canada. A technical meeting to review a draft of this book was held in Lima and Urubamba in October 2002, with the participation of Carlos Abeledo, Keith Bezanson, Barry Carin, KunMo Chung, Janet Maughan, Geoffrey Oldham, Hebe Vessuri and Amitav Rath, all of whom provided valuable suggestions. I am thankful to Leslie Kenny of the Global Studies Center at the University of Victoria, Canada, for her most helpful editorial suggestions.

During the last 30 years I have written and published a number of papers, articles, monographs and books on science, technology and development. Preparing this book has involved a considerable effort to select and synthesize a large amount of material. In addition to Fernando Prada, Ursula Casabonne and Mario Bazán, the research assistants who have helped in the preparation this book, during the last two decades I have benefited from the support of several outstanding young scholars in reviewing and processing source material. Among these, I would like to mention Eliana Chrem, Gonzalo Alcalde, Michael Colby, Gregorio Arévalo, Juana Kuramoto, Fernando Hesse, Carlos Paredes, Gonzalo Garland, Cecilia Cook, Rubén Berríos, Alberto Pascó-Font and Javier Escobal.

Introduction

> The gods condemned Sisyphus to eternally push a rock to the top of a mountain, whence the stone would fall back of its own weight. They had thought, with some reason, that there is no more dreadful punishment than futile and hopeless labor ...
>
> (Albert Camus, *The Myth of Sisyphus*, 1942)

Sisyphus was 'the craftiest of men' according to the ancient Greeks. His cunning, his lack of scruples and the ingenuity of his deceptions infuriated the gods, who punished him for his trickery by endless labor in the underworld. Raising a stone towards the top of a hill only to see it roll backwards seems the epitome of futility, yet Camus's essay on the myth of Sisyphus – written as World War II was raging – raises the intriguing possibility that, ultimately, Sisyphus was a happy man, identified with and fully accepting his apparently hopeless task.

Building science and technology capabilities in developing countries appears to be a Sisyphean task. Time and again investments are made, people are trained, institutions are built, and policies are designed and implemented – often with considerable effort – only to see them fall apart and disappear without trace. Jorge Sábato, the Argentinean physicist who pioneered science and technology policy studies in Latin America, used to say, 'It takes 15 years of hard work to build a world-class research facility, but only two years to destroy it' (personal communication). Developing country policy-makers and politicians, many of whom are unaware of the ways in which science and technology contribute to improve the human condition, have frequently adopted policies and taken decisions that destroyed research and innovation capabilities built over many years of hard work. Thus the pertinence of the Sisyphus myth to characterize what has happened and is happening in Africa, Latin America, the Middle East, South and South-East Asia, and even countries in Eastern Europe and the former Soviet Union, as science and technology capabilities built over decades erode and vanish.

But there is more. Even if our scientific and technological Sisyphus were to reach the top of the hill and, resolutely defying the Gods, managed to stay there, he would only see other hills to climb awaiting him. Hard-won achievements in building science, technology and innovation capabilities appear diminished – perhaps insignificant – as the furious pace of advance at the frontiers of scientific research and technological innovation makes evident the widening chasm between what most developing country researchers and innovators accomplish with great effort, and what their developed country counterparts appear to do with relative ease.

Perhaps, as Camus has suggested, attempting an impossible task makes Sisyphus proud and even happy. Indeed, the manifest futility of the attempt to catch up with the leading scientific and technological nations liberates us from the fear of failure. Moreover, what may appear to be minor achievements against the backdrop of the swift displacement of the science and technology frontier can yield substantive benefits for people in the developing regions. It is in this sense that efforts to build domestic capabilities to generate, acquire and utilize knowledge become crucial to improve the human condition. In addition, the fact that a handful of developing countries have managed to build advanced research and innovation capabilities in just a few decades is a source both of comfort and inspiration.

This Sisyphean challenge is the subject of the present book. The main argument is that developing countries – where more than three-quarters of humanity lives, mostly in poverty – must judiciously invest scarce resources to build their capacities for creating, acquiring and utilizing scientific and technological knowledge, and that this should be done without ignoring their heritage of indigenous knowledge and techniques. As the scientific and technological hills to climb will continue to proliferate – making Sisyphus's task even more daunting – it is also essential to devise ways of keeping the rock on the top of the hill, of preventing the results of past capacity building efforts from being wiped out.

But how to mobilize knowledge to improve the human condition? How to face this Sisyphean task with aplomb and a sense of – why not? – resigned and even fatalistic optimism? This book attempts to answer these questions. It offers a set of concepts for examining the interactions between knowledge, innovation and development, for exploring how to create science and technology capabilities in different types of developing countries, and for placing the role of international science and technology cooperation in perspective. It builds on a large body of work of literature accumulated during the last several decades, and particularly on a series of papers, monographs and books I have written since the early 1970s.[1]

The book is aimed at all persons interested in the role that modern science and technology play in human affairs, to students of the relations between knowledge and development, and particularly at policy- and decision-makers in the public, private, civil society and academic sectors concerned with the disparities between rich and poor countries. The approach adopted has been highly eclectic, drawing from many disciplines (history, economics, sociology, engineering, political science, philosophy), from personal experience (as researcher, advisor, consultant, manager, policy-maker, teacher) and from the contribution of many colleagues from around the world. The general idea has been to produce a short introductory text that could provide an overview of the many different issues related to the Sisyphean task of building science and technology capabilities in the poor countries.

Following this introduction, the first chapter presents a conceptual model that, starting from an account of the diffusion of Western science, provides an integrative framework for relating knowledge, technology and production, and also for attempting a redefinition of what is meant by 'development'. The second chapter contains a historical overview of the interactions between knowledge, technology and production during the last several centuries, as well as a brief account of the way they relate to each other at the beginning of the 21st century. The third chapter characterizes the main features of the 'knowledge explosion' that has taken place during the last three decades, focusing on the way in which research, innovation and the techno-economic paradigm have evolved recently.

The fourth chapter deals with the 'knowledge divide' that has emerged between rich and poor countries and, using the material of the preceding chapters together with statistical information, develops a composite index of 'science and technology capacity' to place countries along a continuum and to classify them in four broad categories. The fifth chapter focuses on the strategies and policies appropriate to create and consolidate science and technology capabilities in the different types of developing countries, and on the role of international cooperation. A few concluding remarks and suggestions for future research complete the book, which is complemented by two appendices and a bibliography.

As the sources of material for this book are numerous, references have been kept to a minimum and are provided in the text only when the ideas can be traced specifically and exclusively to a particular author. The bibliography contains the main sources consulted during the preparation of this book.

Although it builds on a large body of my previous work, and particularly on research supported by the Carnegie Corporation of New York, this book has been prepared during 2002–03 as part of a joint project between FORO Nacional/Internacional–Agenda: PERÚ in Lima, Peru, and the Center for Global Studies at the University of Victoria, British Columbia, Canada. The Rockefeller Foundation provided support for the joint project, which led to the preparation of this book and to the compilation of an inventory of international science and technology cooperation programs.[2] The participants in a technical workshop held in Lima and Urubamba in early October 2002 provided most valuable suggestions and comments on a first version of this book (see the acknowledgements in the preface).

The challenge of pulling together a large body of work into a short book has been most difficult and stimulating. I hope the result offers some ideas and encouragement to those facing the Sisyphean challenge of mobilizing knowledge and innovation to improve the human condition in the 21st century.

NOTES

1. See the bibliography for a list of this material.
2. The inventory can be found at http://www.globalcentres.org/html/project1.html.

1. Knowledge, technology and production: a conceptual framework

This chapter introduces a set of basic concepts that will be used throughout the book. It begins with a discussion of prevailing views regarding the diffusion of Western science and then proposes an integrative framework to view the interactions between knowledge, technology and production and service activities.

1.1   THE DIFFUSION OF WESTERN SCIENCE

In a well-known and widely influential paper George Basalla[1] proposed a conceptual framework to explain the spread of Western science throughout the world. His model consists of three partly overlapping stages. In the first stage, the non-scientific or pre-scientific society of the developing world constitutes a source of problems for European science to delve into; in the second, there is an incipient development of what Basalla calls 'colonial science'; and in the third stage, developing countries struggle to establish an independent scientific tradition of their own.

During the first stage, a few European scientists visit the new lands, explore and collect fauna and flora, study the geographical and physical characteristics of unexplored areas, and then return to their place of origin to complete their scientific work. In their relatively tranquil home academic settings, they put forward their theories and describe their empirical findings.

A dependent 'colonial science' emerges in the second stage. Natural history continues to be the main focus of interest and attention, but the range of scientific activities and problems studied begins to expand until it almost coincides with that of the colonizing power. The colonial scientist is dependent in the sense that the sources of his education and training, the origin of the scientific traditions that he adheres to, the orientation of his activities and the ways of obtaining recognition for his work, are all defined in the metropolitan scientific power and not in the country or region in which he lives and works.

The transition from the second to the third stage is complex and difficult to characterize. Basalla suggest that the stage of colonial science contains, in embryonic form, some of the essential aspects of the third phase. During this transition, the colonial scientist – even though he still gets support from outside – begins to create institutions and traditions that eventually will be the base for an independent scientific culture. Thus, in the third stage, colonial scientists are gradually transformed into scientists whose main allegiance is to their place of origin.

Basalla's model has been rather attractive and widely known, but has two important limitations. First, the use of the concept of 'dissemination' of Western science as the exclusive focus of his analysis, without giving sufficient attention to the processes of 'absorption' and 'internalization' of scientific activities in developing countries. Second, it considers only the diffusion of Western science, without examining the worldwide expansion of the technological base and the internationalization of production activities.

To privilege the concept of dissemination entails adopting an exceedingly Eurocentric perspective, in which Western science, nurtured by different currents of speculative, theoretical and empirical thought that converge upon it from various regions, irradiates the whole world until it displaces the local 'pre-scientific' forms of thought. In reality, what happened – and continues to happen – in different parts of the world, each of them with their own tradition and culture, has been a process of interaction between the imported scientific knowledge and the traditional modes of speculative thought. The permanence of non-scientific forms of speculative thought is a constant in the history of Africa, India, China, Latin America, the Middle East and even Japan, and the interactions between the Western view of the world and a variety of traditional perspectives have taken a multiplicity of forms.

For these reasons, rather than focusing just on the 'diffusion', it would be more appropriate to refer to the 'diffusion, absorption, and reinterpretation' of modern science, admitting that this is a process still under way, that in many parts of the developing world it remains at an incipient stage and is proceeding slowly, and that in some instances there has been little interaction, but rather a juxtaposition of two different and independent forms of thought: the scientific view of the West and the traditional or indigenous perspectives of the developing regions.

Furthermore, if the diffusion of modern science is examined without taking into account the parallel processes of dissemination, absorption and adaptation of modern techniques and technologies (in which there were complex and rich interactions between the Western and the indigenous traditions), and without considering the worldwide spread of European production activities (which accompanied the expansion of the capitalist system at the world level), there is the risk of presenting a partial vision, in which the 'diffusion of Western science' is perceived as an independent phenomenon, conditioned only by its own internal logic, and mostly unaffected by the wider social, economic and political forces at play.

1.2 ELEMENTS OF AN INTEGRATIVE CONCEPTUAL FRAMEWORK

The alternative view of the emergence and diffusion of modern science in the developing countries offered in this book considers the process of generation, transmission and utilization of knowledge in a comprehensive manner. For this purpose, it is possible to distinguish a set of three components that, together with their interrelations and their context, configure an integrative conceptual framework to account for the way in which modern knowledge, technology and production activities spread throughout the world.

The first component is the *evolution of speculative thought* which seeks to generate knowledge to understand natural and social phenomena, and also to offer explanations that give sense to human existence. The second component is the *transformation of the technological base* that provides every human group with a set of organized responses to confront the challenges posed by the physical and social environments, and also with the criteria to select the most appropriate among these responses. The third component is the *expansion and modification of production activities,* which provide goods and services to satisfy the needs of a community and of the individuals that compose it. These three components, considered in a dynamic fashion as continuously changing currents, are linked to each other through institutional arrangements, and are immersed in the broader social, cultural and political context that envelopes human societies.

At a given time and place, a social group can be characterized by the way in which these three currents unfold and relate to each other, by the form in which these currents are linked with their counterparts in other societies and by the specific nature of the interactions between these three currents and the institutional and social environment in which they are immersed.

Although the Western worldview cannot be considered as the privileged or unique frame of reference to examine the achievements of the great diversity of human societies, because of its success in the material and intellectual realms, the West wields enormous influence throughout the world – to the extent that it implicitly provides a yardstick to view the relative standing of other societies. However, in order to highlight the extraordinarily diverse ways in which human beings think and act, and also the enormous potential that this diversity embodies for the future of humanity, it is necessary to move away from the powerful shadow cast by the dominance of Western concepts and things.

The development of the different civilizations and societies in the last several centuries should be seen as a complex whole, whose components are in continuous action and transformation, and in which a perspective – the Western one – came to influence all others. At the same time, other cultures preserved their individuality, influenced Western civilization, and gave rise to new hybrid forms of conceiving the world and relating to it. The image of all civilizations and cultures of the world converging to the culmination and greater glory of the West, implicit in the metaphor of different cultures as tributary rivers that converge on the sea of Western civilization, is rather biased and Eurocentric.[2]

When displacing the perspective of Western civilization as the privileged frame of reference to appreciate the march of other cultures, there still remains the problem of posing a direction for the process of social evolution that could provide a backdrop for comparative studies, and for avoiding the potential excesses of cultural relativism. Two options emerge in this regard. The first is to posit a broad vision of the future direction for the evolution of humanity, which should be acceptable to many different cultures and societies. One leading candidate is the process of 'emancipation' from the forces of nature and from the dominance of other individuals. Emancipation is defined as the capacity of human beings – considered both as individuals and groups – to forge their own destiny and to realize fully their own potential. From this perspective, emancipation would be a key value and an end in itself, and the process of development as the gradual, but not necessarily linear, advancement towards this end.[3]

A second option is to view human evolution as the open-ended process of creating and realizing new values (as well as reinterpreting and realizing old ones), and of continuously articulating shared perceptions of what humanity is and should be. Implicit in this approach is the acceptance of human diversity as a source of potential new values, and the need to agree on ways to reconcile different perceptions of the human condition. This, in turn, requires recognizing that values can be in contradiction, that there is a need to agree on ways of resolving value conflicts, and that openness, tolerance and respect for the views of others are a prerequisite for shared value creation and realization. From this perspective, development may be seen as the complex and arduous process of devising the means for creating and putting shared values in practice.

Development, whether conceived as advancing towards emancipation or towards the creation and realization of values, requires that human societies continuously improve their understanding and mastery of the phenomena that affect them. For more than three centuries, and in spite of limitations that have become evident as we enter the 21st century, modern science has been shown to be the most efficient way of generating knowledge to improve our understanding. Research and the systematic examination (*logos*) of the repertoire of responses available to act upon natural and social phenomena (*techné*) have given rise to a vast array of technologies to confront the challenges posed by these phenomena. Production and service activities associated with modern science-based technologies have acquired an enormous potential to satisfy all kinds of human needs.

As a consequence, development becomes an impossible task without a minimum level of autonomous capabilities to generate scientific knowledge, to transform it into technologies and to incorporate these science-related technologies into production and service activities.

From this perspective, it is possible to distinguish between two types of societies. First, those where the evolution of speculative thought led to or embraced modern science, where scientific activities were directly linked with technological advances and where such advancements led to improvements in production and service activities. Second, those in which the process of knowledge generation was not associated with modern science to any significant extent, where the technical base remained largely isolated from modern science, and where production and service activities did not depend on domestic scientific research or technological advance.

Figure 1.1 indicates that a close interaction between science and technology in developed countries nurtured and underpinned the evolution of production activities. Without the capacity to generate scientific knowledge, to transform it into technologies that were used in the production of improved goods and services, these countries could not have achieved their high rates of economic growth and of improvement in living standards. The close and continuous interaction between science, technology and production led to the creation of an *endogenous scientific and technological base*. This consists in the accumulation of scientific research and technological development capabilities that make it possible to generate new knowledge – and to modify, adapt and recombine existing knowledge – which is then deployed to produce goods and services. In turn, through learning-by-doing and learning-by-using, the utilization of knowledge and technologies in the production sector leads to incremental technical innovations, to the further accumulation of technological capabilities and to new areas for scientific research.

Developing countries were not successful in generating such an endogenous scientific and technological base. Their worldviews differed from those of Western societies where science superseded religion and myth as means to generate knowledge for explaining natural and social phenomena. In these countries, God's will and divine interventions, as well as mysterious and mystical forces, continued to structure the relationships between human beings and the natural and social phenomena that affected them. The evolution of their technical base was largely a result of localized trial and error processes, and the transformations experienced by the production system were also the result of slow changes made to adapt to local conditions and demands.

To the extent that developing countries interacted with their Western counterparts during the last five centuries, they acquired a thin layer of modern scientific, technological and production activities that usually remained isolated from each other. Traditional practices were employed in most production

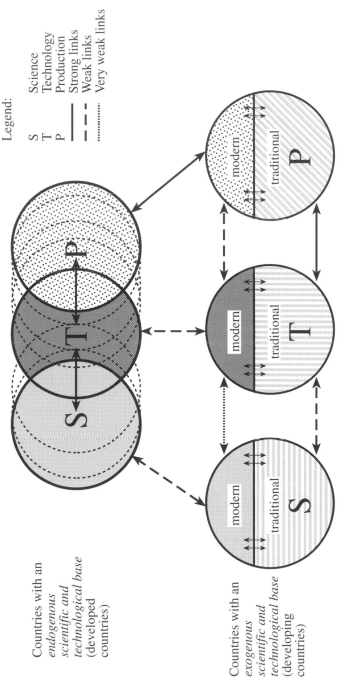

Legend:

S   Science
T   Technology
P   Production
——— Strong links
– – – Weak links
········· Very weak links

Countries with an
*endogenous
scientific and
technological base*
(developed
countries)

Countries with an
*exogenous
scientific and
technological base*
(developing
countries)

Source: Adapted from Sagasti (1979a, p. 13).

Figure 1.1 Relations between science, technology and production in developed and developing countries

activities, many of which were location specific. With few interactions between modern science and both indigenous and modern technologies, and with very little relation between their modern technological activities and their traditional and modern production systems, these countries evolved an *exogenous scientific and technological base*.

The elements or components of the proposed conceptual framework can be summarized as follows (Box 1.1): three currents of human activities (evolution of speculative thought, transformation of the technological base, modification of production and service activities); the social, cultural and political context, together with the institutional arrangements, in which these three currents unfold; the interactions among these three currents, and between these currents and their counterparts in other societies; a direction for the evolution of human activities (emancipation, value creation and realization, development); and an instrumental condition (to acquire an endogenous scientific and technological base).

BOX 1.1   SOME TERMS USED IN THE DESCRIPTION OF THE INTEGRATIVE CONCEPTUAL FRAMEWORK

Speculative thought refers to a set of concepts, ideas, metaphors, myths and other mental constructs that aim at understanding natural and social phenomena, and also at offering explanations that give sense to human existence. It comprises *scientific knowledge*, which is the result of the rigorous contrast between theoretical constructions and systematic experimentation, and *traditional knowledge*, which emerges out of mythical, magic, religious and non-scientific accounts of natural and social phenomena, is anchored in deep beliefs and is usually not amenable to rigorous and systematic empirical testing.

Technological base refers to the set of organized responses to confront challenges posed by the physical and social environment, and to the criteria and procedures to select the most appropriate among these responses. It comprises *techniques*, which are those responses obtained by trial and error and of systematic but non-theoretical experimentation, and *technologies*, which are those responses resulting from rigorous experiments based on prior theoretical constructions.

Production and service activities refer to those actions that lead to the provision of goods and services to satisfy the needs of a community and of the individuals in it. They comprise both

---

traditional production and services, which evolved in specific sites, are closely linked to local resource endowments, are based on *techniques* and have relatively low levels of productivity; and *modern production and services*, which are logically codified, can be moved from one location to another with relative ease, are based on *technologies*, and are characterized by high productivity levels.

Endogenous scientific and technological base refers to the set of usually well developed and closely interrelated scientific, technological and production capabilities that foster *innovation* and make it possible to provide goods and services in an efficient manner. *Exogenous scientific and technological base* refers to the set of usually rather limited scientific, technological and production capabilities that have little interaction with each other, which are seldom related to the stock of *traditional knowledge, techniques and production* in the country, which have relatively stronger ties with their counterparts in the developed countries, and which do not foster *innovation* or efficient production.

Innovation refers to the introduction of new approaches, methods, processes, inputs, resources and other elements – based in large measure on the results of recent or older scientific and technological research – into production and service activities. The adjective 'new' may be assessed against the background of different geographical settings, giving rise to local, national, regional or international innovations.

Source: Prepared by the author.

The unfolding and deployment of these components over time characterize the historical development of societies, help to understand the current worldwide distribution of scientific and technological capabilities, and suggest possible avenues towards development and the acquisition of an endogenous scientific and technological base. The next chapter summarizes briefly the evolution of speculative thought, the transformation of the technological base, the expansion and modification of production activities and the institutional arrangements that support them, highlighting the way in which they have interacted during the last several centuries.

NOTES

1. See Basalla (1967).
2. According to Alvares (1979, p. 2):

   > Human history may be better described not as a movement of different peoples towards some convergent mythical future (although at different speeds and in distinct groups), but as the experience of many discontinuous cultures, each in itself equally important as exhibiting the variability of products of human inventiveness, each crystallizing a system of meanings irreducible to the others.

   Ortega y Gasset ([1933] 1968, p. 77) has argued along the same lines when he opposes:

   > [the tendency] as spontaneous as excessive, reigning in our time, to believe that in the last analysis there is truly no more than one technique, which is the actual European American technique, and that everything else was just clumsy babble towards it.
   >
   > [It is necessary] to counteract this tendency, and to submerge the technique of the present time as one of the many in a vast and multiform panorama of human techniques, revaluing in this way their sense and showing how to each project and model of humanity there corresponds a particular technique.

3. Wertheim (1974, pp. 40–41) suggests that 'the general tendency of human evolution ... consists in a growing emancipation from the forces of nature ... [and] ... the emancipation from the domination of privileged individuals or groups'. This is similar to Sen's (1999) idea of 'development as freedom'. This concept was used in the Agenda: PERU project, which defined the 'common good' in the following terms: 'Expand as much as possible the options which all Peruvians possess to freely imagine, design, choose and realize their own life projects' (Sagasti, 2001, p. 35).

2. A brief historical perspective

Each of the three currents of the conceptual framework interacts with the other two and with the institutional contexts in which they are embedded, and all of these currents and interactions experience change over time. Nevertheless, amidst this multiplicity of mutually conditioned alterations and considering the long historical period, the main transformation experienced by societies takes place when there are major qualitative changes in the nature of speculative thought and in the process of knowledge generation. These lead to fundamental shifts in the conceptions of humanity and its relation to the physical world, which, in turn, influence the evolution of the technological base and the expansion and modification of production activities. Therefore, changes in the nature of speculative thought may be viewed as being the *primus inter pares*, as the primary ordering component of the conceptual framework.

2.1 THE CHALLENGE OF THE WEST

The evolution of the different societies in the world can be examined in a relatively independent way until the period between the 15th and 17th centuries, in which the knowledge generation process underwent a radical transformation. Before this period, it is possible to examine the historical evolution of the process of knowledge generation, of the technological base and of production and service activities in the major civilizations – European, Indian, Chinese, Andean, Maya, Aztec and Islamic, among others – considered more or less as individual units.

However, the world experienced an irreversible transformation beginning with the scientific and industrial revolutions, which were accompanied by qualitative changes in the technological base and by the international expansion of the capitalist system of production that emerged in Western Europe. After those events it is not possible to consider the evolution of the non-European civilizations, cultures and societies in an independent manner: their study must take into account the challenges posed by the West to them and the responses they generated. The point of inflection coincided with the transformation of speculative thought and the changes that took place in the generation of knowledge as a consequence of the scientific revolution. The transition towards a scientific conception of the world made it possible to link systematically abstract theories with practical experiments to study natural phenomena, to discover laws that organize and rule the physical world, and to derive postulates and norms that increased the power of human beings over nature to a previously unthinkable extent.

In parallel with these long-term conceptual changes and encompassed by them, there were transformations in the technological base, partly derived from an improved understanding of natural phenomena and partly from the systematization of empirical knowledge about techniques developed through trial and error. At the same time, influenced by and enfolded by these transformations in the technological base, production and service activities experienced significant changes during relatively short periods, at least in comparison with the transformations experienced by the two other currents. All of these interacted with the institutional arrangements, norms and values that emerged in the different regions of the world to regulate human affairs.

2.2 THE EVOLUTION OF SPECULATIVE THOUGHT

Throughout history, magic, myth, religion and science have provided different ways of generating knowledge about the physical and social contexts in which human societies evolve. These varieties of speculative thought have also attempted to explain the place that humanity occupies in the order of things. The knowledge and information they generate reduce the uncertainties faced by individual and social groups in their dealings with the physical and social environments.

All societies have had their own myths, especially creation myths, which usually explained the relation between human beings and deities, accounted for changes in the seasons and weather, and also provided guidance for the development of techniques and the organization of production. Myths codified knowledge, which before the advent of writing had to be transmitted orally from generation to generation.

Religion superseded myth and provided a more orderly way of accounting for natural phenomena and for explaining the place of human beings in the universe. God's will and divine interventions, which were to be interpreted by shamans and priests acting as intermediaries between deities and humanity, structured the relations between societies and their physical environment, as well as the relations between individuals. The assumption that there exists a natural hidden order, established by divine fiat, would become a motivating force for engaging in speculative thought and for generating knowledge to unveil the mysteries of the universe.

As magic, myth and religion evolved, abstract conceptions began to emerge to account for a variety of natural events and phenomena that were recorded by the senses. For example, since Plato (430–350 BC) and Aristotle (384–322 BC), in the West our changing views of physical reality have evolved largely as a result of the interplay between two realms: an abstract one of ideas and forms, associated with our mental faculties, and a tangible one of matter and substances, associated with our sensory perceptions.

About this time, Chinese scholars and Indian thinkers offered rather elaborate accounts of the structure of matter – the first with five elements, two fundamental forces and a variety of interactions among them, and the second with a more complex and subtle scheme involving minute particles and causal effects – but these conceptions would not affect in a major way the subsequent evolution of Western accounts of physical reality. The Middle Ages added relatively little to the conceptions inherited from Aristotle, and linked them to the designs of an omnipotent God that exerted a continuous influence upon his creatures on earth. Building on Aristotle's conception of matter and forms, Islamic scholars and alchemists developed schemes to link cosmic and earthly forces, and gave accounts of the transformations experienced by minerals and metals.

Abstract thinking led to the development of symbolic logic, geometry, algebra and various branches of mathematics in ancient Greece, India, Islam and other civilizations. Although unevenly developed in different parts of the world, as a whole these advances provided a set of rules for the manipulation of concepts, ideas and other abstract products of the human mind. As a result, it became possible to develop theories and theoretical constructions. With the passage of time the capacity to manipulate abstract symbols would eventually lead to the invention of differential calculus and of other mathematical tools that became essential to the development of modern science in the West.

A variety of institutional arrangements, which took the form of organizations, rituals, social habits and patronage, among many others, were devised by different societies to engage in the production of speculative thought and to generate abstract knowledge. Shamans, priests and clerics, working individually or in sects and churches, applied themselves to the creation, organization and dissemination of abstract notions and concepts that provided accounts of natural phenomena. Kings, tyrants, feudal lords and rulers of all types, as well as public officials and wealthy merchants, gave patronage to those (mostly men) who engaged in the production of knowledge.

The medieval outlook, characterized by the belief that divine will had imposed a hidden order in the workings of the universe which could be uncovered by his creatures, allowed natural phenomena to be seen as following predictable rules to be discovered, rather than as capricious events. Many contributions of the late Middle Ages and the Renaissance laid the foundations for the emergence of modern science in the 16th–17th centuries. These included: the work of Roger Bacon on the importance of rigorous experimentation as a source of knowledge; the rudimentary experiments of alchemists to manipulate the constituent elements of matter; the rediscovery of Aristotle's works through the mediation of Islamic scholars (which would help to break the static, non-experimental hold of Platonic ideas); developments in the plastic arts, which stressed the importance of careful observation and led to the rediscovery of geometry; the invention of Gutenberg's movable type printing press, which allowed a wider distribution of texts that codified existing knowledge; improved techniques of celestial observation (including the invention of the telescope) that, together with advances in mathematics (algebra and geometry), helped to reinterpret existing records and allowed to develop new conceptions of the movements of planets and stars (best exemplified by Copernicus' heliocentric ellipses superseding Ptolemy's geocentric circles with a profusion of cycles and epicycles). All this laid the groundwork for the emergence of the scientific method, which would be developed by Bacon, Descartes, Galileo and Newton.

In the non-Western parts of the world, traditional speculative knowledge confronted the challenge of religious ideas and the intellectual outlook of European missionaries, often with deadly results, as indicated by the movements to 'extirpate idolatries' in Latin America. The interests and preoccupations of European researchers would eventually lead to the rise of 'colonial science' in various parts of the non-Western world.

The emergence of the modern scientific method during the 16th and 17th centuries, which would culminate in the Newtonian synthesis, enabled scientists systematically to relate the realm of ideas with that of tangible biophysical phenomena. The scientific method – characterized by a set of procedures to link the manipulation of abstract concepts and symbols with observations and experiments – led to major advances in all branches of science, from astronomy and mathematics, to physics and biology. The increasing stock of knowledge, a result of the growth of scientific research, generated the need to classify the rapidly growing amount of information and led to the first attempt of French Encyclopedists.

In the two centuries following the scientific revolution science became firmly entrenched as the principal means of generating knowledge. By the end of the 19th century, advances in physics had left prominent members of the scientific community wondering if there was anything else of fundamental nature left to discover. Darwinian evolutionary theory, enriched with Mendel's contributions on genetic factors in inheritance, reigned in the biological sciences and would supply a powerful metaphor for all fields of human activity.

Two major advances in physics in the early decades of the 20th century – general relativity and quantum physics – would alter the prevailing conceptions of the physical world in a fundamental manner. In Einstein's recasting of physical reality, space and time were no longer considered as an immutable, all-encompassing universal stage, independent of the forces and bodies that dwell on it. They were rather conceived as space–time, a four-dimensional construct that interacts with mass and energy. These interactions distort the fabric of space–time and gravity is no longer considered as a force acting between masses at a distance, as Newton had postulated, but as a curvature of space–time caused by the presence of bodies and forces in it.

Quantum mechanics would modify our conceptions of physical reality in an even more radical way. Classical physicists, including Newton and Einstein, considered that it was possible, at least in principle, to define the state of a mechanical system with precision, subject only to measurement errors. The quantum conception of the universe introduced the idea of probability into the basic structure of matter and energy. It was no longer possible – not even in principle – to know with certainty both the position and the momentum of a particle at a given instant in time: Heisenberg's uncertainty principle states that the more precise the measurement of the position, the less exact the measurement of its momentum must be.

However, it would take several decades until these two scientific discoveries would encounter practical applications. Einstein's formulations, complemented with contributions from many other physicists, would eventually lead to the construction of the atomic bomb during World War II, and quantum mechanics would provide the theoretical foundations for the invention of semiconductor devices, which in turn would pave the way for advances in microelectronics and the information revolution in the second half of the 20th century.

During the early decades of the 20th century there were also significant advances in the medical sciences, which included the discovery of antibiotics to treat infections, the use of safe procedures for blood transfusion and the discovery of painkillers such as Novocain. In addition, modern statistical methods were developed starting in the second decade of the 20th century to extract information from physical, biological and social data. These included sampling methods, test of hypotheses and the development of mathematical functions to describe the various properties of statistical distributions. These methods became indispensable tools for scientific research, for they allowed researchers to extract the maximum possible amount of information from limited data, thus facilitating the process of accepting or rejecting hypotheses in scientific experiments and tests.

This brief examination of the evolution of speculative thought suggests that every civilization has its own characteristic way of generating and acquiring knowledge. However, over time and across cultures, a transition can be observed from the contemplation and passive acceptance of the manifestations of nature towards greater interaction between human beings and the phenomena that surround them. With variations in approach, rate of advance and emphasis, changes in speculative thought and in the way of generating knowledge in different societies exhibit a gradual if uneven progression towards the use of reason as the principal means to structure the appreciations of the physical, social, intellectual and, to a lesser extent, spiritual world. Yet, the exercise of human reason can adopt a multiplicity of forms and should be seen from a broad perspective that transcends the narrow vantage point of Western science, whose limitations have led to a revaluation of traditional and indigenous ways of generating knowledge.

2.3   CHANGES IN THE TECHNOLOGICAL BASE

Throughout history each society has developed a distinctive set of responses to relate to its biophysical environment. Agricultural practices, irrigation schemes, animal husbandry, metalworking, pottery-making, manufacture of textiles, stone-cutting, means of transport, production of artifacts, construction methods and health care procedures, among many others, have evolved gradually over long periods of time as social responses to the specific demands imposed by the biophysical context.

Technical responses can be seen as evolving through a series of steps. Initially, a social group has at its disposal a layer of passive empirical knowledge that offers responses only to specific challenges and situations one by one; later it acquires a base of empirical knowledge that begins to detect variations in the efficacy of such responses and to register them through trial and error. At a following stage, it develops a base of active empirical knowledge in which there is the beginnings of systematic experimentation, but without theoretical knowledge to orient the experiments. While advancing in the transition towards more complex and richly endowed sets of techniques, the variety of available responses increases continuously and creates a vast 'genetic reservoir' of technical knowledge.

A subsequent stage is characterized by the evolution of technical responses based on theoretical constructions, heralding the transition from 'technique' to 'technology'. At first such abstract theories are quite rudimentary, and the incipient technologies associated with them are not much different from those derived from the systematization of active empirical knowledge. Gradually, starting in the 15th–17th centuries, theories begin to explain the workings of techniques and anticipate their evolution. Much later, and particularly in the Western world, theory would take precedence over practice. The manipulation of abstract symbols would eventually lead to the development of new technologies lying outside the scope of prior empirical knowledge or experience, and also to their validation through scientific experimentation. The rise of engineering practices and the institutionalization of the engineering profession, particularly after the 17th century, are associated with the triumph of technology over technique.

The institutional arrangements for the transformation of the technological base in the Ancient World and the Middle Ages were closely tied to the organizations involved in the modification and expansion of production activities, for evolution through trial and error requires engaging in actual production. In addition, as technique began to metamorphose into technology, a set of 'common sense' habits of thought and social practices provided criteria for selecting among the rapidly increasing set of potential technological responses. Faced with a growing stock of information about possible ways of dealing with the challenges of the physical and biological environment, societies developed institutional mechanisms – organizations, rules and regulations, selection criteria – that provided guidance in the process of transforming potential into actual responses, thus guiding the evolution of technologies and by extension of production activities.

Technical knowledge, which by the late Middle Ages had been accumulating mostly as a result of trial and error and of systematic but non-theoretical experimentation, began to grow and diffuse rapidly throughout the world. The European discovery of new lands, peoples, plants, animals and products stimulated the search for and exchange of knowledge about techniques and products. In the late 16th century, Francis Bacon would argue that three technological breakthroughs – gunpowder, the compass and the printing press – had changed the course of human history. Advances in military engineering, with the construction of fortresses, bridges and mechanical weapons, and in civil engineering, with the construction of palaces, churches, houses, irrigation schemes and water supply systems, spread rapidly as designs and blueprints became widely available and as engineers began to travel extensively.

Several treatises on agriculture, mechanics, metallurgy, medicine and alchemy (the precursor of chemistry) circulated extensively among practitioners and made knowledge and information, once jealously guarded, available to a growing number of practitioners. As the economic value of such technological advances became evident, the first attempts at creating what are now known as 'industrial property rights' emerged with the establishment of a rudimentary patent system, first in Venice and then in other Italian and European cities. At the same time, a gradual replacement of sources of power took place as advances in technological knowledge led to the development of windmills and watermills that replaced human and animal power, and eventually to the steam engine and various mechanical devices that increased the efficiency of motor power in the late 18th century.

The first ideas for the design of calculating machines, which would replace routine human intellectual labor, were put forward by Blas Pascal in the 1640s, and a rough design for the construction of a general purpose computing machine was advanced by Charles Babbage in the 1830s. Yet, although mechanical calculating machines became a common sight in the late 19th century, it would take another hundred years before Babbage's designs could be realized and a programmable computer would become a practical proposition.

Progress in military, naval, civil and mechanical engineering would gradually become associated with advances in physics and mathematics. The invention of infinitesimal calculus by Gottfried Leibniz and Isaac Newton provided the mathematical tools for solving complex problems, such as computing the trajectories of moving bodies subject to acceleration. The rise of engineering sciences would expand considerably the range of technological knowledge in European empires and in some of their colonies. The importance awarded to modern science and technology was underscored by the privileged position they were awarded by the Founding Fathers of the United States of America at the time of independence.

Thus, between the 17th and 19th centuries, advances in technological knowledge led to a variety of ways of augmenting human capabilities, both physical and intellectual. To a growing extent, progress in technology during this period began to be linked to advances in the sciences, thus laying the ground for the full emergence of science-based technologies in the late 19th and 20th centuries.

By the end of the 19th century, the new applications of electricity and of chemical synthesis were rapidly transforming the technological base in the more advanced industrial nations. The interpenetration of science and technology continued at a rapid pace, particularly in the chemical industry, as advances in organic chemistry led to the development of plastics, pesticides, synthetic fibers, many of them derived from oil (whose production increased significantly). Advances in physics and metallurgy led to improved steelmaking and metalworking technologies.

During the first decades of the 20th century deliberate research efforts transformed knowledge into a critical factor of industrial production, and industrial laboratories began to produce a stream of inventions that soon found their way to mechanical shop floors and chemical plants. Standardization and manufacturing with interchangeable components led to major increases in productivity, and industrial organization methods – pioneered by Frederick Taylor and his 'scientific management' – made further efficiency improvements possible.

Electricity and hydrocarbons became the main sources of power for industry, transportation and households. The increased availability of electric motors, which became smaller, cheaper and more efficient, together with improvements in transmission networks, enabled the wide distribution of electric power at low cost. A similar development took place with the internal combustion engine, which, together with the increased availability of oil and gasoline, led to the spectacular growth of the automobile industry in the second and third decades of the 20th century. In turn, this led to major changes in the production and distribution of all types of goods, in the organization of private life, and in war-making.

The rise of the automobile industry, which was dependent on the almost limitless supply of oil and gasoline at rather low prices, led to the development of vast networks of roads, first in the United States, then in Europe and subsequently throughout the world. In turn, this required networks of gas stations, mechanical repair shops and of suppliers of various ancillary goods and equipment for automobiles. As automobiles became more affordable but still exceeded the capacity of most households to pay for them in full, consumer credit lines began to be offered by financial institutions, an innovation that would soon extend to other consumer durable goods.

New equipment and machinery for industry (machine tools), agriculture (harvesters and tractors), construction (bulldozers and concrete mixers), mining and oil (drilling bits and tools) and administrative tasks (electric calculators and typewriters) led to major improvements in productivity in practically all sectors of the economy. The aircraft industry began in the early years of the 20th century and in just a few decades airplanes introduced fundamental changes in long-distance transport of mail, passengers and cargo, and also in the ways of fighting wars. Technological innovations in telecommunications and in the recording of voice, sounds and pictures transformed human interactions and provided new means for storing and transmitting vast amounts of information across time and space.

With the growth of science-based technologies, technological knowledge began to permeate production and service activities in the industrialized nations and to almost completely replace the technical knowledge acquired through trial and error. Yet, in most parts of the world outside Europe and North America, traditional techniques would still provide for many decades the means to ensure the livelihood of most people in the poor regions of Asia, Africa, Latin America and the Middle East. Even in the industrialized countries, pockets of artisan and 'handmade' production activities remained highly valued and their products were sought after.

This brief review of the transformation of the technological base indicates that the challenges posed by the biophysical environment condition the demand for technical and technological responses and the organizational forms that societies adopt to confront them. Although the transition from technique to technology took place mainly and most successfully in the West, non-Western cultures and societies also acquired and evolved a set of technical and technological responses of their own, usually appropriate to their context, often based on mixes of indigenous and Western knowledge, and always processed by the social organization forms particular to them. As the pre-dominant stock of Western technological responses begins to be questioned, largely on environmental and social sustainability grounds, it would be useful to study the alternative configurations of the technological base in societies that have not been completely Westernized, and where indigenous knowledge and techniques still play a significant role.

2.4 CHANGES IN PRODUCTION AND SERVICE ACTIVITIES

The modification and expansion of production activities has as its principal motivation the satisfaction of the needs of the members of a society. Over time, all social groups have increased the range of products and services provided to their members, enhanced their quality and improved production methods. The exchange of knowledge and information – primarily through trade, the displacement of persons and, later, the transmission of texts and electronic data – has played a major role in the process of producing more goods and services of better quality and with less inputs. However, the definition of needs varies over time, with the degree of material development of a society and with income distribution patterns. Following the logics of the market and of capital accumulation, at present a large number of 'needs' are generated artificially by advertising and propaganda, particularly in highly industrialized market economies.

The expansion and modification of production activities has been closely related to the evolution of the accumulation process, and to the way in which the economic surplus was appropriated, distributed and allocated to various social activities. The traditional uses of accumulation – characteristic of most civilizations and societies until the expansion of European capitalism – include securing food stocks and reserves; constructing temples, palaces and defense walls; waging war and maintaining armed forces; supporting religion and the priesthood; and providing patronage to the arts, crafts and the pursuit of specu-lative knowledge. The new uses of accumulation began to spread during the late Middle Ages and the Renaissance, and were consolidated during the ex-pansion of the European empires and the spread of the capitalist mode of production. These include: opening commercial routes, discovering natural resources, increasing labor productivity, facilitating economic transactions and creating or acquiring technological knowledge. The surplus accumulated in capitalist societies was invested to generate additional economic surplus, which would be used once more for furthering the accumulation process.

Production and service activities grew through the 15th–17th centuries in close connection with the evolution of the repertoire of technical and technological responses. Indeed, before the advent of 'technology,' the tightly joined evolution of technical knowledge and production activities made it rather difficult to distinguish between them. After the marriage of *logos* and *techné*, the range of potential responses to the challenges of the biophysical and social environments increased to such an extent that only a gradually diminishing proportion of these responses were put into practice. A variety of institutional arrangements, mostly related to market forces and the allocation of financial resources, would filter the growing stock of potential technological responses and select those relatively more efficient or profitable to be put into practice.

A counterpoint between the range of products and services, on the one hand, and of needs to be satisfied, on the other, has been an intrinsic feature of the expansion and modification of production in all societies. Needs have spurred human ingenuity to devise new products and services, together with the techniques and technologies associated with them. As new products and services became available, and as new knowledge and information increased the potential supply of goods and services, a corresponding growth and diversification of needs would transform itself into actual demand for such goods and services.

A wide variety of institutional arrangements were devised by different civilizations to organize the production and distribution of goods and services. While self-regulating markets have come to be seen in modern times as the natural way of engaging in such activities, for most of history and in most of the world, reciprocity and redistribution arrangements, usually articulated and mediated by hierarchical authorities, provided the institutional underpinnings for economic transactions in traditional societies.

Over time, the exchange of goods and services began to be structured through markets, which evolved from trading posts along the main trade routes, towards the convergence of sellers and buyers at specific places, such as bazaars and fairs, and towards the creation of self-regulating markets for exchanging symbolic representations of the actual goods. A variety of complementary institutions evolved over time to structure the organization of production and service activities. Property rights and contracts allowed economic agents to receive the benefits and pay the cost of their production and service activities. As the geographical scope of exchanges of goods and services expanded, market transactions superseded the small community of personalized trade and kinship-based connections that embodied trust relations. Impersonal exchange with strangers required other mechanisms to curtail opportunistic behavior and make market transactions reliable.

Many different institutions, some related to incipient state organizations and others to private associations, emerged in the late Middle Ages to provide the public goods – means to validate and enforce contracts, information on the past behavior of economic agents, agreements on trading rules, standards regarding weights and measures, information on the terms of previous transactions – required for the proper functioning of self-regulating markets and for reducing transaction costs. Similarly, going well beyond the widespread use of money as a means to facilitate market exchanges, financial and insurance institutions were created to allow transactions that spanned long distances or occurred over a long period of time.

As a consequence, production activities expanded and diversified at an unprecedented pace at the time of the Renaissance and during the centuries that followed. Improved means of transport increased trade and led to greater specialization and division of labor between economies in Europe and in other parts of the world.

Surpluses obtained from trade, agriculture and the colonies began to be channeled into new production ventures, often through incipient financial institutions. As early as the 13th century, Italian merchants had begun to open accounts with one another to reduce the costs and risks of paying with coin. Bills of exchange were issued authorizing the seller to draw down on the buyer's account at a particular time. As this practice spread, deposit-taking merchants engaged in transactions with various sellers and buyers realized that they did not need to maintain in full the amount of financial resources associated with specific transactions. Idle balances could be used to purchase bills of exchange at discount from sellers who wanted their money before the specified time, thus allowing the deposit-taking merchant to reap the difference between the full and discounted amounts. From these beginnings, a full range of banks and other financial institutions emerged gradually to finance trade and investments in production facilities.

As requests for funding from potential producers and traders grew, those individuals and firms engaged in the provision of financial resources faced the problem of selecting among competing requests for funds. In this way, banks gradually transformed themselves into project selection entities that decided on the allocation of financial resources, primarily on the basis of information about the expected returns from each venture. The worldwide expansion of colonial empires increased significantly the availability of financing obtained from trade surpluses, and this increased the importance of banks as financial intermediaries to the extent that they were able to finance, not only production and commercial enterprises, but also wars and expeditions undertaken by states.

Production and service activities experienced profound transformations during the 18th century, particularly with the Industrial Revolution that started in England and then spread through Europe. The factory system, which was first established in the textile industry, began to expand into other areas of manufacture. The institutional transformations that accompanied the Industrial Revolution required that large-scale, self-regulating markets for labor, land and money be established. These nation-wide markets emerged first in England, and required the forceful intervention of the central government to become a reality.

The swift expansion of European empires in Africa, Asia and Latin America made it impossible to consider the evolution of knowledge production, acquisition, distribution and use in these regions, together with the institutions associated with these activities, without reference to the West.

The repertoire of European technical and technological responses, particularly in the military field, would prove overwhelming to African, Indian, Meso-American, Andean, Chinese and South-East Asian civilizations. At the same time, the exchange of plants and animals expanded considerably agricultural activities in Europe and the conquered lands. Production and trade in the colonies and in far-flung trading posts was organized as a function of the requirements of the European powers, as indicated by the spice trade, the mining of gold and silver, the establishment of plantations and large farms, the trade in textiles (cotton, silk and wool) and the infamous slave trade. In each of these regions, traditional knowledge and institutions did not disappear completely and, in many cases, such as the Andean region, China and India, they have coexisted uneasily for centuries with their transplanted counterparts from the West. In contrast with the colonized lands, Japan adopted policies that allowed it to remain relatively isolated from European influence through the mid-19th century, when deliberate efforts were made by the Meiji dynasty to acquire Western knowledge and technology, and to adapt Western institutions to the Japanese setting.

The emergence of two new sets of industrial activities in the second half of the 19th century – electricity and organic chemistry – signaled the transition towards science-based production in the industrialized nations. This would become a prominent feature of the evolution of knowledge and information during the 20th century, as production and service activities derived from scientific discoveries and technological advances increased in number and pervasiveness.

Beginning in the mid-19th century, agricultural technologies also began to experience major transformations, particularly in the United States with the establishment of the Land Grant Colleges and a network of experimental agricultural stations and of extension services. Medical sciences, technologies and practices, which had experienced major advances through improved anatomical descriptions and the use of the microscope in the 17th–18th centuries, would undergo a further jump in the 19th century with the development of vaccines, the germ theory of disease and the use of anesthetics.

In manufacturing, following the seminal description and explanation of the impact of the division of labor provided by Adam Smith in the late 18th century, the advent of time and motion studies pioneered by Lillian Gilbreth, and rigorous scheduling procedures, initially put forward by Henry Gantt, led in the late 19th century to the development of industrial engineering and of scientific management (as Frederick Taylor would call it two decades later). Thus the methods of science began to be applied, not only to the development of technological knowledge for production, but also to a wide variety of production management, administration and coordination activities.

Towards the end of the 19th century, a broad process of integration into world markets was well under way in most regions, even though trade patterns were highly asymmetric. The more industrialized nations of Europe and North America exported manufactures and other knowledge-intensive goods and services, while colonies in Asia, Africa and the Middle East, as well as the independent nations of Latin America, exported mainly primary commodities. World War I, the Great Depression and World War II interrupted this integration process, and at the same time created the conditions for the development of production activities outside Europe and North America. Developing countries enjoyed a certain degree of 'natural protection' for their industrial activities, as the production systems in the industrialized countries turned to the war effort in 1914–17 and in 1939–45, and also as their production activities experienced a major crisis during the Great Depression of the 1930s. For example, Latin America and India took advantage of this by putting into practice import substitution strategies that led to industrial expansion to supply domestic demand.

This brief review of changes in the social organization of production, which are a consequence of the way in which surpluses are used and of the direction taken by the accumulation process, interact with the transformations of the technological base and the evolution of speculative thought. The expanded repertoire of technological responses presents the production system with a range of possibilities for increasing the generation of surplus, while the greater availability of financial resources constitute a challenge to human inventiveness and stimulates the development of new technologies and the evolution of new forms of speculative thought. The emergence of the secular concept of reason, the desacralization of nature, and the rational conception of the world that found its expression in thinkers like René Descartes and Francis Bacon, provided the ideological foundations for the organization of production in accordance with the demands of the process of accumulation, and also with the private appropriation of the surplus associated with the emergence of market economies. At the same time, the diffusion of capitalist production, characteristic of the industrial civilization of the West, contributed to the predominance of the secularized and instrumental vision of 'rationality', which expanded its scope relentlessly.

A constant in the process of evolution of production activities, particularly during the last four centuries with the diffusion of capitalism and the industrial civilization of the West, has been the enlargement of their geographical scope. From their organization at the local level, production and service activities extended at the regional and continental levels, and at present encompass the whole planet. This internationalization process has been accompanied by the emergence of a global consumer elite with rather similar consumption patterns, which is superimposed over a variety of local forms of consumption in developing societies that correspond to much lower levels of income and resource use.

2.5   INTERACTIONS AMONG THE CURRENTS: THE 'TRIPLE CRISIS'

The interactions between the different stages in the evolution of these three currents – speculative thought, technological base and production activities – visualized against the background of social, political and cultural institutions, characterize the degree of development of a particular society. For example, in the West the evolution of speculative thought led to science as the key method for generating knowledge, which accelerated the transformation of the technological base and fostered the transition from technique to technology, while receiving at the same time the assistance of many technological advances (such as improvement in observation instruments) that contributed to the expansion of scientific research. Production and service activities found increasing support in the new science-related technologies, and at present production activities that employ technologies of scientific origin are clearly superior and dominate the economic scene. All of this took place together with the acceleration and reorientation of the process of accumulation and with the emergence and expansion of capitalism as the dominant mode of production, a process that fed on technological and scientific advances and which, in turn, gave the stimulus and the material resources to support the research activities that generated such advances. This is what led to the emergence of an *endogenous scientific and technological base* in the highly industrialized countries.

In parallel, other cultures and societies developed their own ways of linking these three currents and of relating them to their social, political and cultural contexts. For example, Chinese scholars made great advances in speculative thought and in knowledge about celestial and physical phenomena, Chinese artisans and skilled workmen created techniques based on the systematic application of general rules (as shown by their clock-making proficiency), and Chinese philosophers and administrators evolved social organization forms – such as the imperial bureaucracy – to rule a vast and diverse empire. However, a variety of social, economic and political factors, which emerged as a response to the specific environment of Chinese culture and civilization, were not conducive to modern science and to the creation of an endogenous scientific and technological base. Similar considerations can be applied to India, the Islamic world and to the indigenous civilizations and cultures of other regions such as Latin America and Africa.

The interactions between the three currents are highly complex and difficult to trace, among other reasons because they move at different speeds and their mutual conditioning takes place within different time horizons. Considering a historical period of several centuries, the major qualitative changes in the nature of speculative thought and in the process of knowledge generation will determine the overall direction for social evolution. As a result of these changes, the conception of human beings about themselves and about their relation with the biophysical world is transformed, and the emerging conception gradually permeates and encompasses all human activities, and particularly the technological base and the structure of production activities.

At the other extreme, considering the relatively short span of several decades, the structure of production and service activities plays the key role in shaping social behavior. It defines the specific products and services available to the community, the orientation of the process of accumulation and the distribution of the social product. In this regard, the dominant form of speculative thought, which emerges as the result of an evolutionary process taking several centuries, would constitute a 'fixed' background against which the relatively short-term modifications in the structure of production activities take place.

The time span in which the technological base experiences major transformations occupies an intermediate place, somewhere in between the several decades necessary for the emergence of significant changes in the structure of production activities and the several centuries required for the evolution of the dominant forms of speculative thought. A period between one and two centuries appears appropriate for bracketing the major transformations in the technological base, which define the repertoire of responses available to confront the challenges posed by the physical and social environment. Furthermore, although these transformations take place within the framework of a particular dominant form of speculative thought, they also influence its evolution. At the same time, the prevailing technological base sets the scene for the changes in production and services.

Thus the three currents evolve at different speeds, with the changes in production activities crystallizing in a span of decades, with the transformations of the technological base taking place in a period of between 100 and 200 years, and with the evolution of speculative thought experiencing major changes in a span of several centuries. The modifications in the structure of production and service activities generate tensions that accumulate and pressure

for changes in the technological base; in a similar way, the transformations of
the technological base generate and accumulate tensions that induce fundamental changes in the nature of speculative thought. Therefore, any account
of the evolution of these three currents must take into consideration both their
internal dynamics and the set of reciprocal influences among them. In addition, the time span chosen to frame a particular inquiry will define which of
the three currents plays the dominant role.

Societies experience a period of instability and adjustments when making
the transition from one to another structure of production activities, a process
that takes place every several decades and can take about 20 years. Greater
disruption and instability can be expected when there are major changes in
the technological base, which occur every century and a half or so and take
place over a few decades. Finally, profound upheavals, turmoil and turbu-
lence accompany the transition from one to another dominant form of
speculative thought every several hundred years, a process that can take a
century or more.

The beginning of the 21st century is a particularly complex and difficult
period, in which humanity as a whole is experiencing fundamental changes in
the dominant mode of speculative thought, the technological base and the
structure of production activities. In the first of these, we are in the early
stages of the transition to a post-Baconian age, which is opening the doors to
new forms of knowledge generation that will eventually complement and
possibly supersede science. The technological base has experienced major
alterations with the emergence of a new set of responses, based on the
manipulation of digital information, to respond to the challenges of the
biophysical and social context. Production and service activities are in the
middle of the transition from a techno-economic paradigm based on cheap oil
and energy as the key input, into one where the microchip holds center stage.
Because of the simultaneity of these transitions, we are witnessing a veritable
knowledge explosion whose manifestations will be discussed in the following chapter.

These simultaneous processes of transformation in the three currents have
acquired the character of a 'triple crisis' that is affecting all of humanity to an
unprecedented degree. Their impact has been heightened by the accelerated
process of globalization, and by the emergence of a fractured global order
during the last quarter of the 20th century (see Chapter 5, section 5.1).

3. The knowledge explosion and its manifestations

The triple crisis at the beginning of the 21st century is closely associated with the simultaneous transformations of speculative thought, the technological base and the structure of production, and with an explosive growth in the generation and utilization of knowledge based on scientific research. This has led to the emergence of the 'knowledge society', the twilight of the Baconian age and the transformation of scientific research, highly complex and systemic innovation processes, a change in the structure of production activities and a transition towards a new techno-economic paradigm, and to a recognition of the importance of traditional knowledge, techniques and production. Each of these will be discussed in turn.

3.1 THE EMERGENCE OF THE KNOWLEDGE SOCIETY

Scientific advances and technological innovations are at the root of the complex processes of social change that have taken place during the second half of the 20th century. An inflexion point in the growth of human capabilities to understand the biophysical and social context, and to devise effective responses to the challenges posed by them, can be identified around the time of World War II.

Throughout history the capacity to generate and utilize knowledge has been associated, to a significant extent, with the conduct of war. Yet, the scale and impact of the mobilization of science for military purposes during World War II was extraordinary and unprecedented. Major advances in physics and engineering led to the construction of the atomic bomb, the development of radar and other electronic devices and of the jet engine and new airplane designs. Scientific research also led to the production of new drugs, to advances in medical treatment and to improved synthetic materials. In addition, there were advances in the management sciences, including operational research and mathematical statistics, and in psychology and the study of group behavior.[1]

The impulse given to scientific research by World War II continued in the years that followed, spurred not only by the cold war, but also by the expanded opportunities for the commercial exploitation of research results. As a consequence, during the past 50 years there have been profound modifications in the way knowledge is generated and utilized, and the products of scientific research and technological innovation have become more tightly bound with and more deeply enmeshed in all aspects of human activity. The growth of scientific research, supported by advances in information and computer sciences, has been primarily responsible for this knowledge explosion.[2]

A 'knowledge society', which is radically and qualitatively different from the agricultural or industrial societies of older times, has emerged during the past few decades. In countries with an endogenous science and technology base, advances in productivity and the 'dematerialization' of economies have reduced the relative importance of agriculture, industry and mining, and the proportion of workers engaged in manual labor to produce goods has steadily diminished. In contrast, the share of 'knowledge workers' involved in education, government and private services, information processing and exchange, media and the arts has increased steadily. Even in the manufacturing industries, the knowledge content of products has steadily increased; for example, about half of the value of a new car lies in design, engineering, styling and related intangible components.

This has introduced profound modifications in the relations between workers involved in the production and distribution of knowledge and those engaged in various forms of manual labor. It has altered their relative status and pay, increased the educational content of jobs, introduced the need for lifelong learning and led to more flexible and unstable employment patterns.

The rise of the knowledge society, the emergence of a wide range of 'knowledge industries' and the growing importance of 'knowledge management', has made it necessary to focus on the great variety of types of knowledge that exist. There is an increasing recognition that knowledge acquired as a result of scientific research is but one of many forms of knowledge and, partly as a reaction to the thoroughly Western character of modern science, there has emerged a renewed interest in non-Western traditional or indigenous forms of knowledge. Scientists from both developed and developing countries have begun to explore in a systematic manner the ways in which these other types of knowledge can complement and enrich the products of science (see Chapter 3, section 3.5).

3.2   THE TWILIGHT OF THE BACONIAN AGE AND THE TRANSFORMATION OF SCIENTIFIC RESEARCH

The knowledge explosion that led to momentous changes in all areas of human activity is one of the main expressions of the success and maturation of the

Baconian program. This program has dominated the speculative knowledge scene during the past four centuries and has been associated with the rise of the West. Its architect, Sir Francis Bacon, philosopher and Lord Chancellor of the British Crown, was and still remains a controversial figure, but he was the first to articulate a coherent view on how to use the power of modern science for the benefit of humanity. Nearly four centuries after he put forward his program, our lives and thoughts are deeply influenced by the visions of this extraordinary man. Two of the manifestations of the success and maturation of this program have been the heated controversy that emerged on the nature of science at the closing of the 20th century (what has been referred to as the 'science wars'), and the major changes that have taken place in the way scientific research is conducted, especially in the most advanced fields.

The Twilight of the Baconian Age

Bacon's program has been defined by philosopher Hans Jonas in the following terms: 'to aim knowledge at power over nature, and to utilize power over nature for the improvement of the human lot'.[3] Several features distinguished this program from other views on the production and use of knowledge that were current in Bacon's time:

- a keen awareness of the importance of appropriate procedures to generate knowledge: scientific method and scientific research;
- a clear vision of the purpose of the knowledge-generating scientific enterprise: improving the human condition; and
- a practical understanding of the arrangements necessary to put the program in practice: scientific institutions and public support.

Later, during the Enlightenment, the idea of indefinite, linear and cumulative human progress would become the driving force of Bacon's program. The combination of these three features with the belief in progress, all of them anchored in the firm conviction that humanity is placed at the apex of creation, gave the Baconian program a powerful and unique character, which allowed it to withstand the test of time and endure till the end of the 20th century.

A fundamental assumption of the Baconian program was that human beings occupy the central place in a God-created universe; in Bacon's view divine intervention awarded humans a privileged position in the cosmos. This belief in our centrality would later be carried over into the secular realm and maintained in practically all narratives of human evolution, even though God would be dispensed with in most scientific accounts of the origin of the universe and of our species.

Bacon's account and interpretation of the myth of Prometheus provides a clear statement of his view that divine intervention awarded us a privileged position. For him 'Prometheus clearly and expressly signifies Providence ... the special and peculiar work of Providence was the creation and constitution of Man', and according to Bacon:

> The chief aim of the parable seems to be, that Man, if we look to final causes, may be regarded as the centre of the world; insomuch that if man were taken away from the world, the rest would seem to be all astray, without aim or purpose ... For the whole world works together in the service of Man, and there is nothing from which he does not derive use and fruit. The revolutions and courses of the stars serve him both for his distinction of the seasons and distribution of the quarters of the world. The appearances of the middle sky afford him his prognostications of weather. The winds sail his ships and work his mills and engines. Plants and animals of all kinds are made to furnish him with dwelling and shelter or clothing or food or medicine, or to lighten his labor, or to give him pleasure and comfort; insomuch that all things seem to be going about man's business and not their own.[4]

The assumption of humanity's uniqueness and superiority, and the centrality we awarded ourselves in the cosmic order, have both come under attack from many fronts. New challenges to our inherited conceptions of reality and of what is to be human have emerged during the 20th century, and especially during the last five decades. As a consequence, we are now being compelled to regard ourselves in a new light: we are being forced to reposition humanity in an ex-centric manner in relation to other living organisms and to the universe we inhabit.

Among the findings that require a reframing of our concepts of human nature and a revision of the postulates of Bacon's program, it is possible to find:

- advances in particle physics, which have changed our ideas of physical reality and the notion that there exists an independent world 'out there', separate from us as observers;
- discoveries in quantum cosmology, which are forcing us to modify our views regarding the origin and fate of the universe, as well as our conception of the place we occupy in it;
- findings about the nature of time, which require that we abandon the idea of an absolute and immutable flow of time as a backdrop to the progress of humanity;
- acknowledgment of the tight coupling that exists between human activities and physical ecosystems, which is forcing us to abandon the idea that nature exists for us to conquer and dominate;
- advances in biotechnology and genetic engineering, which are giving

us the capacity to consciously alter the direction of our own biological evolution;

- developments in artificial intelligence, which have emerged to complement and challenge conventional ideas about the uniqueness of human reason; and
- advances in information sciences and technologies, which are in the process of creating new levels of reality and of fundamentally altering the nature of human interactions.

These challenges are a product of the scientific and technological advances of Western civilization; their combined impact, coming with thunderous force at the beginning of the 21st century, is forcing us to reassess the legacy of the Baconian age. Moreover, the unfolding of Bacon's program, the emergence and spread of capitalism, and the worldwide expansion of Western civilization proceeded hand in hand during the last four centuries. As a result, the Baconian program ended up affecting all other cultures and civilizations in a most significant manner.

In each and every area of human inquiry our knowledge is advancing with such speed that it is nearly impossible to provide an accurate picture of the breadth and intensity of the changes under way. As a consequence of these advances, we have been compelled to accept strange notions regarding the probabilistic nature of the physical world, which is no longer seen as something objective and tangible, and to entertain even stranger conceptions postulating that there is a multiplicity of universes whose existence cannot be proved or disproved with the current tools of modern science. We have had to revise our views of linear and absolute time, which can no longer be seen as providing an immutable backdrop for the idea of indefinite human progress. We have also been forced to abandon our human-centered view of the environment, and to renew our ancestors' acceptance of reciprocity linkages between human beings and the biophysical world that surrounds us.

At the same time, we are in the process of becoming responsible for guiding the biological evolution of our species, regardless of our readiness to accept such awesome responsibility. We have had to face the challenge of artificial intelligence, which has shown us that the capacity to reason is not an exclusive prerogative of human beings, and we have also been forced to cope with the swift emergence of cyberspace, a new level of reality, which has challenged the dualism that underpinned the modern scientific outlook. Last, but not least, we have realized that technological advances in information technologies are intensifying and transforming human interactions, fragmenting our selves and profoundly altering our sense of personal identity.

These challenges make it necessary to reconsider the foundations and main premises of the Baconian program. The methods of modern science have evolved gradually since the time of Bacon, Descartes, Galileo and Newton, but are poised to experience even more significant transformations during the 21st century. Our efforts to improve the human condition have had a host of unintended negative consequences, which have made it impossible unambiguously to abide by Bacon's injunction to employ knowledge for the benefit of humanity. The institutional settings for the generation and utilization of knowledge, together with the idea of public support for research, are experiencing wrenching transformations, as private firms and market interests penetrate the hallowed halls of basic science. In addition, confidence in the steady and indefinite character of human progress has been badly shaken by the human catastrophes of the 20th century (World War I, the Great Depression, Nazism, the Holocaust, World War II, post-cold war genocides). Rather than being at the center of the universe, humanity is now seen as occupying an insignificant place in the cosmos, and as the result of a most improbable string of coincidences that led to the emergence of life, sentient beings and our species.

All of this suggests that, as we enter into the 21st century, we are witnessing the maturation and incipient twilight of the Baconian age. The challenges to Bacon's program and the assaults on the centrality of humanity, as well as our attempts to cope with them, are creating confusion, anxiety and a widely shared feeling that humanity has lost its bearings. The progressive loss of the ethical and moral dimensions that Bacon had built into his program may be seen as one of the reasons for the paradox that the program's success ended up undermining its own foundations.

One manifestation of such confusion is the 'science wars' debate of the 1990s, which have pitted practicing scientists against students of the conduct of science. These debates have been seen by some academics as following from the earlier controversies spurred by the publication, four decades ago, of C.P. Snow's book *The Two Cultures and the Scientific Revolution*,[5] which focused on the different perspectives, methods and social impact of science and the humanities. The radical critics of the scientific enterprise on one side of the science wars debate (postmodernists, feminists, radical sociologists) argue that science is socially constructed, that the knowledge it generates is not inherently objective and thus not superior to other forms of knowledge. In consequence, the results of scientific research should be viewed and treated no differently from other forms of knowledge generated by history, literature, the humanities or the social sciences.

These views are not representative of researchers in the wider field of science, technology and society studies, in which historians, sociologists and anthropologists, study the conduct of science in a rigorous and systematic way. However, they may be seen to emerge naturally out of this field of inquiry, which aims to apply the methods of science to the study of the conduct of science itself. In this way, as the Baconian program reaches its full deployment and maturation, the conduct of science has acquired a self-reflective character and the scientific method is being used to scrutinize the practice of science itself.

The response of many physical and biological scientists has been to reject the relativist claims of the radical critics and, in some cases, to argue that scientific truth has an intrinsically objective character and that scientific research is not affected by extraneous factors. More moderate voices acknowledge social and institutional influences on the conduct of science, particularly in the choice of research topics, the formulation of hypothesis and adoption of a research approach, but assert that scientific findings have a privileged place in relation to other forms of knowledge – primarily because of their verifiable character and their widespread practical applications.

Modern science is also being challenged by religious fundamentalists, who argue the supremacy of knowledge as revealed by the particular divinities associated with their creeds. Perhaps the most serious threat to a secular and reason-based view of the world and of humanity at the beginning of the 21st century comes from the Christian 'creationist' movement in the United States, where some states have mandated their educational systems to treat both evolution and creationism as hypotheses on the same level. In other parts of the world the scientific outlook is under siege by religious fundamentalists who reject its association with everything they find odious or objectionable in the West. Still other, more moderate, critics of Western science argue that alternative ways of conceiving biophysical phenomena and human interactions – associated with traditional and indigenous forms of knowledge and cosmologies – should be recognized as having validity and usefulness, rather than being considered as backward and rejected out of hand by the scientific community.

The Transformation of Scientific Research

The last decades of the 20th century have also witnessed major transformations in the conduct of scientific research. The first of these refers to the multiple and complex interactions between scientific research, technological innovation and the commercial exploitation of research results, which are now characteristic of the most dynamic sectors of the world's economy. These interactions have shown the inadequacy of a linear conception of scientific and technical progress, in which scientific findings lead directly to new technologies that can be subsequently incorporated into production and service activities. Instead, the accumulation of technological innovations provides a base of observations for science to delve into, and technological

progress plays an important role in defining the agenda for scientific research. Innovations in industry, agriculture, mining, energy, transportation,
education and health care, among many other fields of human activity, continuously identify new problems to be addressed by science. At the same
time, new instruments for observing, measuring and testing biological and
physical phenomena have become a major determinant of scientific progress.

All these interrelations have dramatically reduced the time between scientific discovery and economic exploitation of research results. During the 19th
century it took 50 years between Faraday's discovery that a moving magnetic
field can produce electricity and the first practical system for the generation
and distribution of electric energy. Forty years elapsed between Einstein's
early 20th-century discovery of the fundamental relations between matter and
energy and the detonation of the first atomic bomb. Twenty years were
necessary for Watson and Crick's discovery of the structure of DNA in the
mid-20th century to be applied in the first transplant of genes. Yet, it took
only six years between the discovery of the electron tunneling effect by Esaki
in 1957 and the first commercial application of semiconductor diodes. The
time between the creation of new knowledge and its incorporation into new
products and processes has been shortening very rapidly, particularly in the
fields of information technologies, biotechnology and new materials.

A second transformation refers to the institutional settings for the conduct
of basic research, applied research and for the development of science-based
products and processes. Shifts in funding sources and the more prominent
role of the private sector in the conduct and financing of scientific research
are behind these institutional changes. In most of the high-income countries
the private sector is now responsible for conducting at least half of research
and development activities (in Japan, Sweden, Finland and Ireland the proportion is even higher). Universities account for 15 to 20 per cent and public
research institutes are responsible for the rest. Moreover, in addition to their
own research and development activities, private firms also finance research
in universities and work jointly with government institutions.

As a result, links between universities and private firms are strengthening,
collaborative industrial research and technological alliances have become an
imperative in the more advanced technological fields, and venture capital
firms and some specialized government agencies are playing an increasingly
important role in providing capital for new-technology businesses. These
changes have been taking place during the last three decades and primarily in
the high-income countries, although several newly industrializing nations –
particularly in South-East Asia – are also moving in this direction. This new
situation stands in marked contrast to the estimates provided by J.D. Bernal
for the United Kingdom in the 1930s, which indicated that private industry
accounted for 25 to 30 per cent of research expenditures.

Institutional settings for the conduct of scientific and technological activities have also changed largely in response to major increases in the cost of basic and applied research, which are also bringing about greater concentration in fields where large facilities are needed and results may take a long time. Certain fields of inquiry (experimental particle physics, genetics, molecular biology and astrophysics, among many others) have become increasingly dependent on high-cost instruments, which – as in the case of chemical synthesis and advanced microelectronics research – combine advances in electronics, materials sciences, optics, analytical techniques and information processing.

The consequences for developing countries of the maturation of Bacon's program and of the changes in the conduct of scientific research are quite significant. While the twilight of the Baconian age will last for a rather long time, spanning at least the first half of the 21st century, it is not too early to begin the search for a new program to replace the one articulated by Bacon nearly four centuries ago, but one in which all civilizations and cultures may see their heritages and contributions reflected. Without falling into the excesses of religious fundamentalism and radical postmodernism, it is necessary to frame the achievements of Bacon's program, of Western civilization and of modern science, in a broader framework that should leave room for other perspectives to complement and enhance the scientific outlook of the West.

The implications of the transformations of scientific research are more immediate and direct. The high cost of advanced instruments and financial constraints have effectively put many fields of research out of the reach of the vast majority of scientific institutions in developing countries. At the same time, advances in information technologies may be ameliorating some of these trends. First, relatively inexpensive 'virtual' advanced instruments can be replicated by using software that runs on standard personal computers, and it has been pointed out that the virtual version of an instrument, which is often more versatile, can cost 20 times less than a conventional scientific instrument.

Second, advances in microelectronics, information processing and telecommunications now allow researchers from all parts of the world, including the poorer regions, to actively participate in joint research projects. There is greater access to libraries and other sources of written information, it is possible to interact in real time with peers in distant places through electronic conferences and there is also the possibility of sending data and test results to centers with advanced facilities to analyze them. While these opportunities are still being explored, there is a great potential for developing country scientists to become actively involved in many aspects of scientific research, even in areas such as theoretical physics that would appear at first sight closed to them.

Finally, the accelerated pace of scientific progress requires a continuous effort to keep up with advances in the state of the art, for the stock of knowledge and the capabilities acquired through training and research become obsolete rather quickly. The Sisyphean nature of the process of building endogenous science and technology capabilities is a direct consequence of such acceleration. These needs and trends have important implications for human resources development and for training researchers in advanced scientific fields, particularly in the developing countries where highly qualified professionals are in short supply.

3.3 THE SYSTEMIC NATURE OF TECHNOLOGICAL INNOVATION

In parallel with the transformations of scientific research, and closely associated with the changes in the technological base, the nature of the innovation process has changed significantly: it has acquired a more complex and systemic character, particularly in science-intensive industries. Innovation has now become more expensive, requires greater sophistication in management techniques, gives rise to new forms of appropriation of technological knowledge, intensifies both international collaboration and competition, and has also transformed the role that governments play in support of innovation.

The systemic nature of the innovation process is manifested in at least three ways: the emergence of new technologies as a result of the convergence of advances in rather different fields, the complementary character of specific technical advances required to materialize a particular innovation, and the larger network of institutions and support services necessary for innovation to take place.

First, while innovation was seen until recently as a process of pushing the frontiers of a particular technological field or trajectory, during the last three decades a host of innovations have emerged largely as a result of combining and integrating very different technologies. It is anticipated that this process of technological intermingling and fusion will continue and accelerate in the first decades of the 21st century, and that a host of new technologies will emerge out of it. Box 3.1 presents a speculative account of the future interactions of four broad technology fields.

Second, new technologies complement each other and it is seldom the case that individual advances in information technology, new materials, chemical synthesis and biotechnology, among many others, can be applied on their own without complementary inputs from other technological fields. This has become clearly noticeable in automation and computer-aided manufacturing, where microelectronics, computers, telecommunications, opto-electronics and

BOX 3.1   AN ILLUSTRATIVE AND SPECULATIVE
ROAD MAP FOR THE APPLICATION OF
SCIENTIFIC AND TECHNOLOGICAL
ADVANCES IN THE NEXT FIVE
DECADES

Knowledge base	Scientific and technological advances	Multiple interactions	Potential application fields 1–2 decades	2–3 decades
			Biointeractive materials (B1+M2+I2+I3+I5)	
Biological sciences and biotechnologies (B)	B1. Genomics B2. Molecular biotechnologies B3. Agribiotechnology B4. Scaling-up of laboratory biotechnologies B5. Bioenvironmental management		Bionics and biomechanical devices (B2+B4+I3+I4+I5+M2+E2) Cognitronics (I3+I5+M2+E2)	
Information sciences and technologies (I)	I1. Quantum computing I2. Cognitive computing I3. Highly responsive sensors I4. Wireless computing I5. Advanced analytics I6. Combinatorial and simulation methods		Mechatronics (I3+I5+I6+M3+E2) Genotyping (B1+I5+I6) Statistical analysis of massive data (I5+I6+I1)	
Materials sciences and technologies (M)	M1. Nanotechnology M2. Smart materials M3. High-performance materials M4. Advanced catalyst materials		Complex systems management (I2+I3+I4+I5+I6+M2+E2+I1) Biomanufacturing of objects, devices and food (B2+B3+B4+M3+M4) Biofuel production plants (fuel farming) (E3+B3+B4+B5+M4) Environmental and ecosystems protection (B5+I3+I6+E1+E3)	
Energy sciences and technologies (E)	E1. Next-generation conventional fuels E2. Mobile power sources E3. Biofuels		Molecular manufacturing (I1+I5+M1+M2)	Quantum nucleonics (I1+M1+M2+M3)

The table above summarizes popular accounts of the potential applications of several emerging science and technology advances in the coming decades. These are related to four areas of knowledge: biological, information, materials and energy sciences and technologies which, although they do not exhaust the potential sources of knowledge to put into practice these applications (for example, contributions from mathematics and economics are also required), provide a good idea of the convergence and increasing complexity of the innovation process at the beginning of the 21st century. The 12 potential application fields combine, to differing degrees, several of these advances, and they are likely to be deployed sooner or later during the next five decades.

Biointeractive materials. Biologic sensing devices will become small enough to reside on or inside people, animals, and crops. There they can monitor the host's health and even act on problems as they arise, transmitting information or releasing agents to deal with them. They include fabrics that change color when exposed to unsafe chemical or biological compounds. These biosensors could eventually be implanted inside the human body and help repair damaged tissue, such as nanoscale crystals that bind to form synthetic bone.

Bionics and biomechanical devices. These aim at replacing lost or disabled body parts, which represents an extension of existing technologies (pacemakers, hearing aids). This requires developing small, long-lasting power supplies, microchips and new materials that can be safely integrated into the body. For example, electroconductive plastics that take orders directly from the brain may be used to replace muscles and create prosthetic arms and hands.

Cognitronics. The aim is to develop reliable and removable interfaces between the brain and electronic devices such as computers. While efforts in this field are still primitive, a combination of advances in sensor technologies, new materials, advanced analytical methods and brain research, may yield significant progress and lead to the development of such interfaces in the not too distant future.

Mechatronics. This refers to the integration of familiar mechanical systems with new electronic components, advanced sensors and intelligent software to improve the efficiency of machinery and equipment, including automobiles, power generation plants, machine tools, internal combustion engines and electric motors. The aim is to reduce waste and pollution, improve performance and develop new mechatronic applications for activities that require greater precision and accuracy than current mechanical devices.

Genotyping. Mapping the human genome will allow us to link diseases to specific genes, a feat that has been accomplished in a partial manner by merging advances in the biosciences with information technologies. While much more work remains to be done for this field to lead to safe and reliable disease prevention and health preserving technologies, it is likely that practical results will be achieved within one or two decades, and that they will spawn complex ethical, legal and institutional challenges.

Statistical analysis of massive data. This refers more to a research method than to a field of technology applications. It involves the combination of advances in statistical methods with massive computing power to process and extract information from huge amounts of data. Already in use to a limited extent in data mining and simulation, this will lead to new ways of examining complex interactive phenomena, such as climate change and the behavior of economic systems, and of developing scenarios and other planning tools.

Complex systems managements. The growth and unpredictability of large interconnected systems, such as the Internet, power generations and distribution, air traffic control, global financial markets, urban transport, natural disasters prevention and relief activities, and institutional arrangements for detecting and preventing the transmission of infectious diseases, require highly sophisticated management and control procedures. The convergence of advances in sensors and data-gathering devices, wireless computing, analytical methods, simulation techniques, mobile power sources and smart materials together with progress in mathematics, statistical methods and software will open up new avenues for the monitoring and control of complex systems. Eventually, quantum computing may provide a new means for real-time management of even more complex systems that may require large-scale virtual reality simulations.

Biomanufacturing of objects, devices and food. The idea is to go beyond the chemical and mechanical manufacturing plants and to use biological processes and organisms to produce a large variety of objects and devices, and also of food products. This is already happening in some cases (for example, in vaccines), but advances in molecular and agribiotechnologies, the scaling up of laboratory procedures and the availability of new materials for reactors and catalysts will expand biomanufacturing to new fields and reduce its cost.

Biofuel production plants. The objective is to replace oil with fuels – ethanol, methanol and biodiesel, among others – from genetically engineered crops. This will become possible in the near future, but could have negative effects by displacing food production and using scarce water, as well as the dangers associated with the possible uncontrolled dissemination of genetically altered plants.

Environmental and ecosystems protection. The aim is to take advantage of scientific and technological advances across many

fronts to develop applications that will reduce the negative impact of human activities on ecosystems. Bioenvironmental
management techniques based on a better understanding of
complex biological cycles will allow us to target environmental
protection measures more effectively, the use of advanced sensors with very small power sources will allow us to gather data
from remote places, the use of combinatorial and advanced simulation techniques will help process large amounts of information
and predict environmental impacts, and improvements in conventional fuels and biofuels (see above) will reduce the harmful
effect of power generation.

Molecular manufacturing. This aims to build complex structures atom by atom, and involves the convergence of new
materials, nanotechnology, advanced analytical methods and possibly quantum computing. While still a long way off and would
require the development of molecule-size assemblers to initiate
molecular manufacturing and building microscopic motors, scientists have succeeded in positioning individual atoms on a
surface and in building carbon nanotubes whose walls are 10
atoms thick and are from 50 to 100 times stronger than steel.

Quantum nucleonics. Even more speculative than the preceding technology convergence fields, this involves tapping the
energy of the atomic nuclei without resorting to fission or fusion,
and aims at developing a portable, safe and non-polluting source
of nuclear power. If perfected, it could provide a powerful source
of energy that leaves behind no residual radiation. It could also
be used in photolithography to etch circuits onto denser, faster
microchips.

Sources: Saffo (2002), p. 72 (for additional information see: http://www.
business2.com/articles/mag); '10 Emerging Technologies', *Technology Review*,
February 2003, pp. 33–9; Brockman (2002).

artificial intelligence are fusing together into an integrated technology system, as well as in fields like aircraft production, biosynthetic materials and
the development of new drugs and treatments.

The technological convergence implied by the more systemic character of
innovation has made it necessary for leading firms to develop expertise in a
broader array of technologies and scientific disciplines, as evidenced, for
example, by the need for the food processing and pharmaceutical industries
to develop competence in biotechnology, molecular biology and advanced

electronic instrumentation. It also has implications for the concept of critical mass in research and innovation, for in addition to quantitative critical mass (amount of resources, number of people) and qualitative critical mass (type of resources, personnel qualifications, nature of facilities), it becomes necessary to acquire an 'interface critical mass', which refers to competences and capabilities in fields that are adjacent or indirectly related to the one in which the particular innovation is focused.

Third, the increasingly systemic character of innovation is also reflected in the larger number of actors that take part in the process of bringing major innovations to the market and the users. In addition to the firms and government agencies directly involved in this process, there may also be subcontractors, suppliers of inputs and equipment, laboratories and other organizations that provide technological services, legal and technical advisors in intellectual property rights, management consultants, educational and research institutions, marketing research units, distributors and trading companies, financial institutions and venture capital firms. All of these are complemented by various government agencies and departments engaged in the formulation and implementation of policies that affect the innovation process, either directly or indirectly. The concept of 'national systems of innovation' was advanced in the 1980s to account for the growing complexity of the institutional arrangements, legal frameworks, incentive systems, strategies, policies, practices and attitudes required to bring about the innovation process.

The systemic character of innovation has several consequences that affect the way in which policies are designed and implemented, the cost of innovation, the pace and geographical spread of changes in production systems, and the demands it imposes on management capabilities and infrastructure facilities.

The growing complexity of the innovation process requires that a distinction be made between 'explicit' science and technology policy instruments, which directly influence decisions regarding innovation, and 'implicit' policy instruments that affect them indirectly through the creation of a conducive environment, or through second order effects of other policies and decisions made by private firms, government agencies and academic institutions. These implicit policies influence the conduct of scientific research and of technological innovation, but lie outside the conventional boundaries of science and technology policy. They include financial, credit, educational, labor, tax, trade and regulatory policies, among others. In consequence, to promote innovation it is not enough to focus on explicit policies, and it becomes essential to harmonize these with a wide range of implicit policies to ensure they reinforce and not cancel each other.

Another consequence of the more complex and systemic character of innovation has been a steady increase in the cost of incorporating research results into production and service activities, and of bringing new products to the market. The higher costs of innovation and the larger risks faced by firms in a more competitive environment have increased barriers to entry in many fields of industry, particularly in those where government regulation plays a major role. For example, in the pharmaceutical sector the cost of discovering, testing and bringing to market a new medicine may exceed US $500 million and take 12–15 years, while a factory to produce microchip wafers in the late 1990s cost over $1 billion and had an expected lifetime of five years (which means a depreciation rate of about $4 million per week). Paradoxically, the increase in competitive pressures has generated a host of cooperative arrangements between industrial firms, primarily in pre-competitive research and marketing. However, only firms with substantive financial or technological assets (including small firms focusing on specific technology niches) can be expected to become players in the game of international technological alliances.

In addition, new technologies have made it cost-effective to produce more differentiated products and to accelerate innovation by adopting shorter product cycles. Flexible automation is lowering the minimum efficient plant size in several industries, and advances in communications and information technology permit adopting a 'just-in-time' approach to production management, reducing inventory costs and requiring close interactions with suppliers and markets. Low labor costs are no longer the dominant criterion to locate production sites, especially for high-end manufactured products, and corporations are finding it more advantageous to establish industrial production facilities close to their markets, suppliers and research and development centers. The result has been that facilities for the production of many manufactured goods and the provision of certain services (for example, electronic durable goods, data processing) have spread throughout the globe.

The more systemic character of innovation requires a greater emphasis on management skills and capabilities. To realize the full potential of new technologies it has become necessary to introduce innovations in organization and management, a task for which advances in information technology have provided many tools. A well-developed physical infrastructure is also required to support innovation, including a good network of roads and transport facilities, telecommunications and data transmission networks, reliable electricity supply, access to waste disposal facilities, and a clean water supply. In addition, it may be necessary to count on advanced repair and maintenance services for a variety of laboratory and industrial equipment. However, the greater complexity of large-scale technological infrastructure facilities also increases their vulnerability and the risk of systemic failure. Risk assessment and management has become essential in large systems such as financial information networks, air traffic control, water supply, and energy generation and distribution.

The changes in the nature of the innovation process have mixed effects on the prospects for developing countries. On the one hand, there is the possibility of incorporating advanced technology components into traditional and conventional technologies, in what is known as 'technology blending', which can lead to more appropriate and higher productivity innovations geared to developing country needs. On the other hand, the comparative advantage of developing countries is shifting away from low labor costs and natural resources, forcing major changes in education, industrialization and environment policies. In addition, the physical and institutional infrastructure required to support increasingly complex innovation processes may well be beyond the existing capabilities of most developing countries.

However, it must be kept in mind that a significant proportion of products and services in these countries are produced, distributed and consumed locally using traditional methods, which eases to a certain extent the pressures exercised by the taxing demands of innovation processes in the more advanced and competitive fields. There are about 2 billion people, a third of the world's population, the vast majority of them living in poor countries, without access to electricity, and for them advanced technology innovation has little meaning. Alternative approaches and policy frameworks are necessary to examine the nature of innovation systems in poor countries facing severe resource constraints.

For example, it may be necessary to devise strategies for the 'management of technological pluralism' in order to take advantage of the broad range of available technological options in specific developing country situations. This implies combining advanced technologies that are based on the results of scientific research, with conventional technologies resulting from the accumulation of research and technical improvements over several decades, and with traditional techniques that are the result of empirical trial and error processes that took a very long time. For this to happen, it is necessary to create conditions for the coexistence of a diversity of traditional, conventional, modern and blended technologies with different productivity levels, labor requirements, energy intensities, environmental impacts and opportunities for learning. Such eclectic combinations of technology are likely to be better suited to local conditions in developing countries.

3.4 THE RESTRUCTURING OF WORLD PRODUCTION AND A NEW TECHNO-ECONOMIC PARADIGM

The maturation of the Baconian program, the transformation of scientific research and the growth in complexity of the innovation process, have all coincided with major changes in the worldwide production of goods and services. These are manifested in a set of changes in the content and distribution of production activities, and in a transition of the dominant techno-economic paradigm that underlies the dynamic sectors of the world economy.

The Distribution and Content of Production Activities

The world production of goods and services has grown at a rapid rate during the past 50 years. The total global output of goods and services at the end of the 20th century was six times larger than that of 1950, and this high rate of expansion is likely to continue during the next two decades. World trade has grown even faster, particularly in goods and services with high technological content.

This growth of production and trade has been accompanied by major shifts in the geographical distribution of production (Table 3.1). The United States accounted for about 30 per cent of world production in 1950, but its share had diminished to around 20 per cent at the end of the 1990s. Europe, Japan and a few emerging economies increased their share significantly, while countries of the former Soviet Union saw their participation in world production drop precipitously in the 1990s. It is expected that the high growth rates experienced by China during the past two decades will continue well into the 21st century, to the extent that the most populous country in the world is likely to overtake the United States as the world's leading producer of goods and services during the next three decades.

The redistribution of production capacity at the world level during the last half of the 20th century has proceeded in parallel with major increases in direct foreign investment, although most of it has been taking place primarily between developed countries. In 2000 these countries accounted for about 70 per cent of total outflows and 80 per cent of foreign direct investment inflows. Moreover, foreign direct investment in developing countries concentrates in about a dozen emerging economies, primarily China, India, Mexico, Brazil and, until recently, Argentina, even though when calculated in per capita terms, this apparently high degree of concentration diminishes significantly.

The reasons for international corporations to invest in developing countries have evolved during the last several decades. In the 1950s and 1960s investments were primarily orientated towards the exploitation of natural resources, while in the 1960s and 1970s a significant proportion was orientated towards import substitution schemes, particularly in the relatively large developing countries where transnational corporations invested to take advantage of domestic markets. From the 1980s onwards foreign direct investment in developing countries focused on establishing export-orientated production facilities in the emerging economies, aiming to achieve greater efficiency and reduce costs in globally integrated production and distribution systems.

Table 3.1 Distribution of world production of goods and services (in percentages)

Country/region	Year								
	1870	1913	1950	1960	1970	1980	1990	1998	
US	8.73	19.00	27.13	23.94	22.05	20.80	19.97	21.93
Japan	2.26	2.53	2.91	4.32	7.14	7.66	8.38	7.53
Western Europe[a]	30.97	30.05	25.38	26.05	25.77	24.03	22.39	20.64
Western offshoots[b]	1.16	2.40	3.20	3.10	3.10	3.17	3.10	3.15
Eastern Europe	13.54	15.50	14.01	14.51	13.87	12.52	10.02	5.32
Latin America	2.55	4.23	7.52	7.78	7.87	9.26	7.70	8.72
Asia[c] and Oceania	37.26	23.98	16.40	16.99	16.92	19.29	25.42	29.63
Africa	3.52	2.31	3.44	3.31	3.28	3.27	3.02	3.08
World	100.00	100.00	100.00	100.00	100.00	100.00	100.00	100.00
World total[d]	1127.90	2726.10	5372.30	8448.60	13 810.60	20 005.80	27 359.00	33 725.90

Notes:
(a) Southern Europe included.
(b) US not included.
(c) Japan not included.
(d) World GDP level in billions 1990 constant dollars. Maddison used a sample of 199 countries up to 1990 and a sample of 217 countries for 1998.

Sources: Maddison (1995; 2001).

Table 3.2   Market shares of exports, 1985 and 1998 (in percentages)

Year	All products	Primary	All manufactures	Resource based	Low-technology manufactures	Medium-technology manufactures	High-technology manufactures
Shares of products in world exports:							
1985	100.0	21.7	73.8	21.1	13.7	30.2	12.4
1998	100.0	11.5	84.2	14.5	15.8	32.8	21.1
Shares of developing countries in world exports:							
1985	24.3	52.1	16.4	26.3	26.7	8.3	10.7
1998	25.0	39.7	23.3	23.7	34.5	15.3	27.0

Note: 'Other' transactions are not shown here, and account for the difference between shares in total exports and in primary plus manufactured products.

Source: Adapted from Lall (2000b), who calculated the figures using United Nations Comtrade data provided by UNCTAD.

The distribution of world exports by sector has also shifted in a major way towards technology-intensive goods, particularly during the last two decades. Table 3.2 shows the shares of different types of products in world exports for 1985 and 1998, and also the proportion of these exports accounted for by developing countries. During this period, the share of primary products was cut nearly in half and the share of high-technology manufactures increased significantly. The proportion of exports of low-, medium- and high-technology manufactures accounted for by developing countries (mostly emerging economies) also grew at a rapid pace, partly as a consequence of the creation of 'global value chains' that involve the establishment of production and distribution facilities in many different countries.

Table 3.3   Evolution of world manufactured exports by technological categories (percentage shares)

Technology categories	Year				
	1980	1985	1990	1995	1996
Resource based	19.5	19.3	15.5	14.0	13.7
Low technology	25.3	23.4	23.7	22.0	21.3
Medium technology	38.6	37.3	38.5	36.9	37.2
High technology	16.5	20.1	22.2	27.1	27.7

Source: Adapted from Lall (2000b), who calculated the figures using United Nations Comtrade data provided UNCTAD.

Considering just manufactured exports (Table 3.3), between 1980 and 1996 the share of resource-based and low-technology manufactures declined as a percentage, while the share of medium-technology manufactures remained stable, and the percentage of high-technology manufactures nearly doubled. This indicates the extent of the shift in the structure of world production and trade in favor of products with a higher science and technology content. Underlying these structural shifts there is a persistent long-term deterioration of the terms of trade between primary products and manufactured goods – with the short-term exception of the 1970s, when the price of oil tripled as a result of concerted action by the Organization of Petroleum Exporting Countries – and also of a deterioration of the terms of trade between industrial commodities (resource-based and low-technology manufactures) and high-technology products.

These shifts in export shares proceeded in parallel with changes in the rules for international trade and finance. Liberalization and deregulation in both developed and developing countries gave a greater role to market forces in determining the volume, content and direction of the international flow of products, capital, technology, information, knowledge and skilled labor. Barriers to trade and investment were dismantled, regulations harmonized and there has been a convergence in national trade and investment policies. However, while tariffs and quantitative restrictions on trade were lowered or eliminated, there has been a slower progress in reducing qualitative barriers to trade, which take the form of standards and various types of certification that products have to satisfy. In particular, environmental regulations and social concerns are becoming barriers to developing country exports. Yet, at the same time, stricter environmental regulations could encourage the use of environmentally friendly technologies, as well as the recovery and upgrading of ecologically sound traditional techniques.

The 'Trade-Related Aspects of Intellectual Property Rights' (TRIPS), which are the subject an agreement administered by the World Trade Organization, are another important feature of the international trade scene at the beginning of the 21st century. The provisions of this agreement will affect developing countries in widely different ways depending on their level of science, technology and innovation capabilities. In general, they are likely to increase the costs of importing technology and increase the bargaining power of technology owners, mostly firms in the developed countries. They also restrict opportunities for reverse engineering, and for copying and adapting technologies, which were key components of the technological development strategies of European countries, the United States and Japan, as well as the newly industrialized countries of East Asia during the 19th and 20th centuries. While more stringent intellectual property rights regulations could conceivably encourage research and promote foreign direct investment, the range of developing countries that can benefit from these is restricted to the emerging economies that already have substantial technological and innovation capacities.

The rapid growth and diversification of financial transactions has been a distinctive feature of the international economic scene during the past three decades. International financial markets now comprise a tight web of transactions involving global securities trading, arbitrage in multiple markets and currencies, futures trading with exotic financial instruments, portfolio investment through a bewildering array of international funds, and massive trans-border capital movements. Financial transactions have acquired a life of their own and have largely become uncoupled from the production of goods and services. For example, currency transactions, which in the early 1970s represented about 10 times the value of international trade, shot up and reached about 70 times that value in the mid-1990s. The number of transactions in financial derivatives linked to interest rates increased from about

1 million in the early 1980s to more than 20 million in the early 2000s. Deregulation, liberalization and the incessant search for higher returns and risk diversification, together with advances in information and telecommunications technologies, have been behind the enormous growth in world financial activities.

The growth and diversification of financial markets and instruments has had an important influence on the creation and acquisition of science, technology and innovation capabilities in countries and corporations. Venture capital firms and specialized government agencies now play a key role in financing scientific research and technological innovation in developed countries and some emerging economies, particularly in the high-technology sectors. From a less positive perspective, the constant search for high returns and risk diversification in a highly complex and volatile international financial context can work against investments to develop innovation capabilities, especially in countries where equities markets are an important source of enterprise financing. The pressures to exhibit short-term returns in order to maintain high equity valuations may shift resources away from the complex and long-term tasks of building technological capacities within the firm, and may not encourage experimentation and risk-taking that spurs innovation.

The structure and content of world production activities have changed radically during the past half-century, primarily as a result of the combined impact of technological advances, institutional changes and modifications in the international policy environment. But these, in turn, have been influenced by the interests of powerful countries and large corporations, which have sought to reap and keep most of the benefits of scientific and technological progress. The dominant position of the United States during this period has allowed it to shape the rules of international trade and finance, to chart paths for the evolution of technologies in most fields, and to push forward the interests of American firms throughout the globe. This has been exemplified by the pressures exerted by the United States government for developing countries to adopt intellectual property rights regulations that favor and reinforce the position of American corporations.

Transition of Techno-economic Paradigm

The changes in the structure and content of world production, as well as the transformation of the production system at the national level, can be interpreted as the latest manifestation of a series of cyclical phenomena that have characterized the history of economic activity during the past few hundred years. During this period there has been an alternation of phases of rapid growth and stagnation giving rise to five 'long waves' with a periodicity of about five to six decades.

The most widely accepted long waves account of economy cycles has been suggested by Christopher Freeman and Carlota Perez, who postulate that the transition from one long wave to another involves changes in the dominant 'techno-economic paradigm'.[6] A techno-economic paradigm is a combination of interrelated product and process, technical, organizational and managerial innovations, which generates significant and sustained increases in potential productivity for all or most of the economy, and which opens up an unusual range of investment and profit opportunities. A major characteristic of the diffusion pattern of a new techno-economic paradigm is its spread from a set of initial industries and services that serve as carriers to the economy as a whole. In the transition from one techno-economic paradigm to another, the production activities related to the old one do not disappear but lose their dynamic character in comparison with those associated with the new techno-economic paradigm.

The organizing principle of each paradigm is to be found most of all in the dynamics of the relative cost structure of all possible inputs to production. In each paradigm, a particular input or set of inputs – the 'key factor' – fulfills the following conditions: low and rapidly falling relative cost; apparently almost unlimited ability of supply over long periods, which is an essential condition for the confidence to take major investment decisions; and clear potential for use or incorporation of the new key factor in many products and processes throughout the economic system, either directly or through a set of related innovations which reduce the cost and change the quality of equipment, labor and other inputs to the system.

The key factor in the techno-economic paradigm that is being superseded is oil, whose falling cost, apparent unlimited supply and widespread utilization reorganized the production of goods and services at the world level from the 1920s onwards. Transport related industries (automobiles, trucks, tractors, aircraft, motorized armaments), consumer durables and oil-based products (petrochemicals, synthetic materials, textiles, packaging), accompanied by the expansion of the physical and institutional infrastructure to make full use of these products (highways, airports, gasoline distribution systems, consumer credit), set the pace for economic growth during what has also been called the 'Fordist mass production wave'. This wave extended through the 1970s, and included the 1950–73 'golden age' of unprecedented world economic and trade expansion.

A new techno-economic paradigm emerged in the 1980s as the microelectronic chip began to replace oil as the key factor. Information and telecommunications industries and services (computers, electronic consumer goods, robots and flexible manufacturing systems, computer-aided design and manufacturing, telecommunications equipment, optical fibers, ceramics, software, multimedia, information services) took the lead in the process of economic growth. Digital telecommunications networks, routers and other special purpose computers, cable services and satellites, whose cost has been dramatically reduced, provide the infrastructure for the rapid expansion of information and communication services.[7]

This transition has profound implications for the way in which production is organized in enterprises, for competitive strategies and for the institutional arrangements to support production and service activities at the national and international levels. The well-proven set of common-sense managerial guidelines, derived from decades of successful experience in increasing efficiency within the framework of the techno-economic paradigm based on oil, is giving way to a new set of efficiency principles and practices associated with the new possibilities opened up by the microelectronic chip. The transition from a mass-production model of organization for production, characteristic of the age of oil and the automobile, to a flexible networks model, which is associated with information technology, upsets the premises of managerial common sense in enterprises. For example, from mass products and standardized markets it is necessary to move to diversified adaptable products and highly segmented markets; rules of operation that focus on 'one best way' of routinely doing things must yield to continuous product improvements and frequent process changes in learning organizations; and centralized structures with hierarchical pyramids, functional compartments and rigid communications channels, must give way to decentralized networks, strategic centers, semi-autonomous functional units and interactive communications. These shifts require fundamental changes in management styles and practices

During the transition from one paradigm to another, the overlap between the mature phase of the old paradigm and the initial phase of the new one provides greater opportunities to secure technological advantages and improve competitiveness. Firms and countries face an unusually favorable situation: a 'double window of opportunity' provides access both to what until recently was privately appropriated knowledge in the fully deployed and mature paradigm, and to what will soon become private appropriated knowledge in the new techno-economic paradigm (Figure 3.1). Usually there are lags in the diffusion of the technological innovations involved in the transition from one paradigm to another, which could extend the time the window of opportunity remains open. This could allow firms in developing countries to enter well-selected markets for products linked to the new technologies, and also to successfully compete in international markets with rejuvenated products associated with the old techno-economic paradigm.

However, to take advantage of the double window of opportunity offered by the change in techno-economic paradigm, firms and countries must be well positioned not only with regard to their scientific and technological

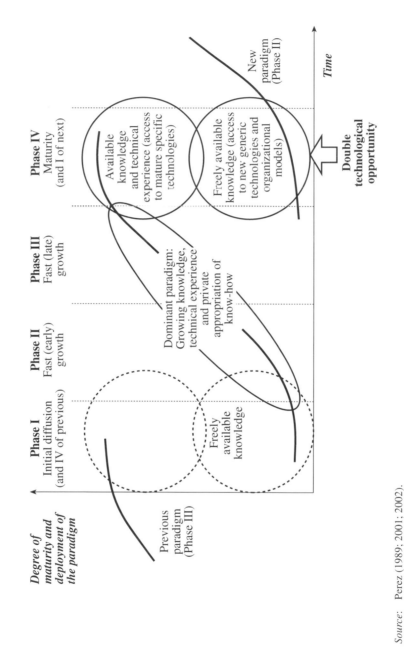

Source: Perez (1989; 2001; 2002).

Figure 3.1 Phases of the dominant techno-economic paradigm

capabilities, but also in relation to managerial skills, institutional flexibility, capacity to adapt, ingenuity and creativity. In the end, those firms and countries that take advantage of this opportunity may not be the most advanced in their scientific and technological capabilities, but those that arrive at the best match between science and technology potential, institutional framework, good governance and social consensus, and where this match is in tune with the international policy environment.

As the new techno-economic paradigm based on the microchip and on the spread of information technologies becomes dominant and moves into phases II and III, the possibility for developing countries to take advantage of the opportunities it offers diminishes. The accumulation and private appropriation of knowledge, technical experience and know-how create barriers for new potential entrants into the various production and service activities associated with the dominant techno-economic paradigm. Building up technical and organizational capabilities to take advantage of new opportunities requires time, particularly in developing countries with weak science, technology and innovation systems. For this reason, it may be pertinent to speculate about the characteristics of the next techno-economic paradigm and to prepare for its emergence. Such speculations are fraught with uncertainty and should be viewed with utmost care, but could nevertheless help envisage the broad range of scientific and technological capabilities that would be necessary to follow up developments in scientific research, technological trajectories, institutional arrangements and social pressures that will lead to the emergence of one or another new techno-economic paradigm.

A scenario-building exercise could help to anticipate the features of the possible key factors that would underpin alternative techno-economic paradigms, as well as the potential carrier industries that would lead to their deployment in the coming decades. It has been suggested that environmental friendly technologies (e.g. new sources of energy) and some aspects of biotechnology (e.g. genetically manufactured organisms) may provide the impetus for the emergence of a new paradigm. The road map in Box 3.1 provides further candidates for these speculations. The main point of such exercises would be to explore what would be necessary to take advantage of the maturation of the dominant techno-economic paradigm as it deploys fully (possibly in the next two or three decades), and also to build capacities to foresee and accompany the emergence of a new techno-economic paradigm, so as to seize opportunities as they emerge.

3.5   TRADITIONAL KNOWLEDGE, TECHNIQUES AND PRODUCTION

The importance of traditional knowledge, techniques and production has been highlighted in the conceptual model of Chapter 1 (Figure 1.1), primarily because in most developing countries they provide the means of subsistence for large segments of the population. Non-scientific modes of speculative thought still play an important role in these countries, the evolution of the stock of techniques has been largely the result of localized trial and error processes, and the transformations of the production system have usually been the result of relatively slow changes made to adapt to local conditions and demand. It has been estimated that more than three-quarters of the world's population relies on indigenous knowledge to meet their medical needs, and at least half relies on traditional knowledge and techniques for crops and food supplies. As about one-third of the world's population does not have access to electricity, all modern technologies and production activities that depend on this source of energy are out of their reach.

Indigenous or traditional knowledge is crucial for survival and for improving the quality of life of poor people. However, such knowledge is rarely codified and systematized – or codified in highly idiosyncratic manners – which makes it difficult to transmit, at least according to modern scientific and technological standards. It therefore depends on its depositaries or users for its diffusion, which usually takes place by imitation, exchanges of goods and the recounting of oral traditions. In many cases, indigenous knowledge, techniques and products have been lost because there are no reliable mechanisms to record and store them, the people that knew about them died and because the dominance and presumed superiority of Western ways have led to their being ignored or discarded. Local specificity is a constraint to their wider application, and even when they might be suitable for transfer to other locations, the limited number of people who know about them and the small scales of production limit their diffusion. These features of traditional knowledge, techniques and production are related to the rationale of pre-capitalist societies in which artisan work and custom-made production are the rule.

A selective screening and upgrading of traditional techniques could enhance their contribution to improvements in living standards and poverty reduction. For this to happen, it is necessary to devise strategies, create institutions and adopt policies to foster a sustained interaction between the depositaries of indigenous knowledge and techniques on the one hand, and scientific researchers and engineers on the other. One approach would be to focus on 'blending' traditional techniques and modern technologies, injecting modern components to improve the performance and increase the productivity of traditional systems of production.

Another approach would involve focusing on the complex interactions that take place within indigenous production systems, attempting to understand their logic and functioning before injecting modern or upgraded indigenous techniques and knowledge components. This leads to the recognition that there exist 'indigenous innovation systems', which evolve and change in response to challenges and stimuli that are different from those of market-based innovation systems. Their distinctiveness is a result of a community's conception of the world and the place of human beings in it, its history of successes and failures with techniques and production (discovery of new plant varieties, crop loses due to bad weather), of institutional factors (collective decision-making, prevalence of reciprocity relations, rigid power structures), accidental discoveries and findings, and of the specific characteristics of the ecosystems in which they live. Participatory research methods, which actively involve the members of the community, may provide an effective way of understanding the logic of these indigenous innovation systems and help to improve their performance.

The different levels of productivity of traditional techniques and modern technologies have significant implications for employment generation. This is important in developing countries with high rates of population and labor-force growth, and where a large proportion of jobs are self-generated. The deliberate management of technological pluralism (Section 3.3) can help to link indigenous knowledge, technology and production with their modern counterparts. In turn, this may help to create an endogenous science and technology base in developing countries, which need not necessarily follow the same trajectory as that of the developed countries of today.

NOTES

1. The nature of this inflexion point has been described by J.D. Bernal in a paper on 'The lessons of war for scientists', when referring to the emergence of 'operational research' as an integrative and practical way of linking the conduct of scientific and technological research to war operations:

    The original implications of operational research are already making themselves felt in peacetime economy. In principle it amounts to the statement that any human activity and any branch of that activity is a legitimate subject for scientific study, and subsequently for modification in the light of that study. Once this is accepted in practice, which implies the provision of research workers to carry out these studies, the way is open to a new level of man's control of his environment, one in which economic and social processes become scientific through and through. (Quoted in Bernal, [1937] 1967, p. xxi)

2. The explosive growth of knowledge has been described by David Linowes (1990, quoted in Dahlman, 1994, p. 2) in the following terms:

It took from the time of Christ to the mid-eighteenth century for knowledge to double. It doubled again 150 years later, and then again in only 50 years. Today it doubles every 4 or 5 years. More new information has been produced in the last 30 years than in the previous 5,000.

3. Jonas (1984, p. 140).
4. Bacon ([1627] 1985, pp. 270–71).
5. Snow (1963).
6. See Freeman (1983), Freeman and Perez (1988), Perez (1989; 2001; 2002).
7. The speed and spread of information technology advances has been characterized in the United Nations Development Programme (UNDP) *Human Development Report 2001* in the in the following terms:

> In 2001 more information can be sent over a single cable in a second than in 1997 was sent over the entire Internet in a month. The cost of transmitting a trillion bits of information from Boston to Los Angeles has fallen from $150 000 in 1970 to 12 cents in 2001. A three-minute phone call from New York to London that in 1930 cost more than $300 (in 2001 prices) costs less than 20 cents in 2001. E-mailing a 40-page document from Chile to Kenya costs less than 10 cents, faxing it about $10, sending it by courier $50 … The Internet has grown exponentially, from 16 million users in 1995 to more than 400 million users in 2000 – and to an expected 1 billion users in 2005. Connectivity is rising at spectacular rates in Europe, Japan, the United States and many developing countries. In Latin America Internet use is growing by more than 30% a year – though that still means that only 12% of individuals will be connected by 2005. (UNDP, 2001, pp. 32, 37).

4. The knowledge divide and disparities in developing country capacities

The impact of the knowledge explosion has been felt throughout the planet, but in a most uneven manner. The capacity to generate and utilize scientific and technological knowledge has become highly concentrated in a few developed countries, while the majority of developing countries still rely on traditional knowledge and techniques, complemented by a rather thin layer of modern knowledge, technologies, products and services, passively received from the technologically advanced countries. This has created a 'knowledge divide' between those parts of the world where science, technology and production are tightly intertwined, and those in which the limited scientific, technological and modern production activities remain apart from each other and where traditional knowledge, techniques and products still play a major role. The knowledge divide has been relentlessly deepening and enlarging, and has led to a sort of 'knowledge apartheid' that radically separates those societies that have an endogenous science and technology base from those that do not.

The explosive growth of information technologies and of the infrastructure to support them has also become a source of inequality between developed and developing countries. The terms 'information poverty' and 'digital divide' have been coined to describe the plight of poor countries with very limited access to the world sources of information, a condition that drastically reduces possibilities, options and choices for development.

Yet, there is also great variation in the level of science and technology capabilities of developing countries. A few have managed to build endogenous science and technology capacities during the past half-century, others have lost the capabilities they accumulated over decades of effort, many have built some capabilities in specific fields, while others have not even begun to create the human resources, institutional, financial and physical infrastructure to support modern science and technology. The interventions that are appropriate for each of these groups of developing countries are quite different, which suggests the need for a classification scheme to guide policy design and implementation (Section 4.2).

4.1   THE MAGNITUDE OF THE KNOWLEDGE DIVIDE

Disparities between science, technology and innovation capabilities of developed and developing countries are much larger than economic disparities. At the end of the 20th century, the ratio between the gross domestic product (GDP) per capita of the high-income countries of the Organization for Economic Cooperation and Development (OECD) to that of the low-income countries (as defined by the World Bank) was about 64 to 1, while the ratios of global national investment per capita and trade per capita were 66 to 1 and 68 to 1, respectively (Table 4.1). If India – with its one billion inhabitants – is excluded from the group of low-income countries, the first and third ratios improve slightly while the second worsens a little. These economic disparities between rich and poor countries have been growing continuously during the last decades: in 1989 these three ratios were, respectively, 62 to 1, 51 to 1 and 30 to 1.

However striking these disparities may be, they are dwarfed by the differences between developed and developing countries in their capacities to generate scientific knowledge, develop modern technologies and to produce high-technology goods and services. The ratio of scientific publications per 100 000 inhabitants in OECD countries to that of low-income countries is 89 to 1 including India in the latter group, but rises to 331 to 1 if this country (which has a large and very active scientific community) is excluded. The ratio between patent applications by residents per 100 000 inhabitants is 197 to 1 including India and 260 to 1 excluding it, while those of high-technology exports per capita are 646 to 1 and 730 to 1, also including and excluding India, respectively.

In the mid-1990s total annual expenditures in research and development by the high-income OECD countries exceeded US$500 billion, a figure greater than the combined GDP of about 80 of the world's poorest countries. Western Europe and North America, together with Japan and the emerging Asian countries, accounted for about 85 per cent of total world expenditures in science and technology; China, the countries of the Commonwealth of Independent States (formerly part of the Soviet Union) and India, accounted for a further 10 per cent, while the rest of the world accounted for only about 5 per cent. Regional differences in research and development expenditures are also indicative of the disparities in science and technology capabilities: Latin America and Sub-Saharan Africa spent about 0.3 per cent of their GDP in research and development, China 0.5 per cent and India and Central Asia about 0.6 per cent, while the US and Japan, with much higher GDPs, spent 2.5 and 2.3 per cent respectively.

The distribution of human resources devoted to science and technology is slightly more balanced than the distribution of science and technology

Table 4.1   Economic disparities and the knowledge divide (1999)

Indicator	Values and ratios				
	(A) OECD countries	(B) Low-income countries	Ratio (A)/(B)	(C) Low-income countries (excluding India)	Ratio (A)/(C)
Gross domestic product per capita (constant 1995 US$)	29 578.0	461.0	64.2	465.8	63.5
Gross capital formation per capita (constant 1995 US$)	6 730.3	101.7	66.2	95.2	70.7
Trade per capita (imports + exports of goods and services) (constant 1995 US$)	13 030.9	190.6	68.4	246.4	52.9
Scientific output: scientific publications per 100 000 inhabitants (1995)	72.9	0.8	88.8	0.2	331.4
Technological output: patent applications by residents per 100 000 inhabitants	75.4	0.4	197.2	0.3	260.0
Production output: high-technology exports per capita	831.6	1.3	645.5	1.1	729.5

Source: World Bank, *World Development Indicators 2001*, CD-ROM:

High-income OECD countries (1999 gross national income above US$ 9266): Australia, Austria, Belgium, Canada, Denmark, Finland, France, Germany, Greece, Iceland, Ireland, Italy, Japan, Luxembourg, Netherlands, New Zealand, Norway, Portugal, Spain, Sweden, Switzerland, United Kingdom, United States.

Low-income countries (1999 gross national income below US$ 755): Afghanistan, Angola, Armenia, Azerbaijan, Bangladesh, Benin, Bhutan, Burkina Faso, Burundi, Cambodia, Cameroon, Central African Republic, Chad, Comoros, Congo, Côte d'Ivoire, Eritrea, Ethiopia, Gambia, Georgia, Ghana, Guinea, Guinea-Bissau, Haiti, India, Indonesia, Kenya, Korea (Democratic Republic), Kyrgyz Republic, Lao PDR, Lesotho, Liberia, Madagascar, Malawi, Mali, Mauritania, Moldova, Mongolia, Mozambique, Myanmar, Nepal, Nicaragua, Niger, Nigeria, Pakistan, Rwanda, Sao Tome and Principe, Senegal, Sierra Leone, Solomon Islands, Somalia, Sudan, Tajikistan, Tanzania, Togo, Turkmenistan, Uganda, Ukraine, Uzbekistan, Vietnam, Yemen Republic, Zambia and Zimbabwe.

expenditures, which reflects the lower cost of highly qualified human resources in developing countries. About 50 per cent of the world's scientists and engineers are concentrated in the OECD countries, 17 per cent in Eastern Europe and in the Commonwealth of Independent States, 15 per cent in India, China and the newly industrializing countries of East Asia, and the rest in the developing regions of Asia, Africa, Latin America and the Middle East. By the end of the 1990s there were approximately 1.1 million scientists and engineers in the United States and 630 000 in Japan, which compares with about 585 000 scientists and engineers in China and 160 000 in India. However, when these figures are expressed in relation to total population, the gap between developed and developing countries becomes evident once again: there were about 4.1 scientists per thousand population in the US, 2.1 in the European Union and 5.1 in Japan, but only 0.54 in China and 0.16 in India.

Scientific research and technological development organizations in most developing countries are highly vulnerable to changes in the domestic economic and political climate, which can affect negatively the slow and arduous process of institutional consolidation, and are also vulnerable to the attraction exerted by better financed and more advanced research and development organizations in developed countries. Building a world-class research institution takes at least a decade and a half of sustained efforts, but these achievements can be destroyed in a couple of years by the emigration of highly qualified staff. As pointed out in the introduction to this book, economic and political instability in many developing countries has made the building of science and technology capabilities akin to mythological Sisyphus' efforts to push a heavy stone uphill. Yet, there is one developing country which has made spectacular gains in human resources capabilities during the last two decades: university enrolment rates in the Republic of Korea rose from 15 per cent to 68 per cent between 1980 and 1997, and 34 per cent of total enrolment was in science, engineering and mathematics – which exceeds the OECD average of 28 per cent.

In some poor regions a university education can be considered as a passport out of poverty. About three-quarters of African and Indian emigrants to the United States have tertiary education, and this proportion is about one-half for China, the Republic of Korea and South America. However, in the case of Korea these emigrants represent only about 15 per cent of the total number of people with tertiary education, and the corresponding figures are about 7 per cent for South America and less than 3 per cent for India. The 'brain drain' of scientists and engineers creates serious problems for the smaller developing countries, but not as serious for those countries in which there is large reservoir of highly skilled potential emigrants. Some developed countries have focused on attracting such qualified persons, and a senior United States government official once stated that, from his perspective, highly skilled people everywhere in the world are the 'common heritage of mankind'.

The distribution of the world's scientific and technological output, measured with the rather imperfect indicators of scientific publications and registered patents, also shows a rather extreme degree of concentration of capabilities to generate modern knowledge and technology. In the mid-1990s, nine high-income countries and India accounted for nearly 80 per cent of world scientific publications, and high-income countries published 25 journal articles for every one of those published by low-income countries. Similar degrees of concentration were found in patent indicators: more than 96 per cent of patents were registered by the United States, the countries of Western Europe and Japan. The United States received 54 per cent of total world royalty and license fees payments, with a further 12 per cent going to Japan.

Access to the rapidly growing world stock of knowledge and information, together with the capacity to screen, select, process and utilize it, have become essential in the process of building endogenous science and technology capabilities. Disparities in access to sources of information are also very large, even in conventional means of communication such as newspapers, radio and telephones. For example, at the end of the 20th century, there were about 600 newspapers circulating daily per 1000 inhabitants in Japan, while the corresponding numbers were a hundred times lower in Bangladesh and 2000 times lower in Burkina Faso (0.3 newspapers per 1000 inhabitants). Moreover, there were only about 30 radio receivers for every 1000 Tanzanians and 80 for every 1000 Indians, but 1000 for every 1000 Canadians.

In 2001 there were 56 telephones per 1000 inhabitants in Africa and 202 in Asia, in contrast with 840 in Europe, 1100 in the United States and 1180 in Japan. Most of the growth in telephone access at the world level, and particularly in developing countries, has been due to the recent introduction of wireless technology. Mobile-phone use grew at an annual average rate of approximately 50 per cent between 1995 and 2001, the number of mobile-phone subscribers increased from about 90 million in 1995 to 946 million in 2001, and about half of the total phone service subscribers in the world now use mobile phones.

Disparities in the number of homes with personal computers and access to the Internet are also very large, and may be widening the knowledge divide between developed and developing countries. There were about 85 computers per 1000 inhabitants at the world level in 2000, but this average hides very wide differences: in Africa there is about 10 computers per 1000 inhabitants, in Asia about 30, and in Japan and the United States the corresponding numbers are 350 and 620, respectively.

The Internet consists of a massive network of permanently interconnected host computers, which route traffic, exchange e-mails and provide information, and of a huge number of temporary connections created by users when they log on with their personal computers. In early 2001 there were about 100 million host computers, a growing number of which are web servers providing information through the World Wide Web. The growth of web servers has been nothing short of spectacular: from 75 000 in 1995 to more than 25 million in 2000. The number of countries connected to the Internet has grown from eight in 1988 to 214 in 2000, and only a handful remain unconnected, primarily for political reasons. However, the limited availability of telephone services in developing countries is a major constraint to growth in the number of users

The number of Internet users in developing countries has grown at about twice the rate of that of developed countries during the last decade, and in 2000 the latter accounted for about a quarter of the 315 million users worldwide. Between 1998 and 2000 the number of users increased from 1.7 million to 9.8 million in Brazil, from 3.8 million to more than 17 million in China, and from 2500 to 25 000 in Uganda. In spite of these high rates of growth in the number of users, disparities between developed and developing countries remain huge. While almost a third of the people in developed countries are connected, less than 2 per cent of the population in the developing countries has access to the Internet. About 80 per cent of Internet users live in the high-income OECD countries, which contain only 15 per cent of the world's population.

These figures provide a snapshot of the huge disparities in the worldwide distribution of science and technology capabilities and of access to information at the end of the 20th century. However, the asymmetries are much greater than these figures would suggest, primarily because of the cumulative character of the processes of building capabilities in modern science, technology and production. As capacities in these fields are acquired it becomes easier to continue accumulating them, and those countries that have a long history of doing so are in a much better position to reap the benefit of future advances in science and technology. This 'Matthew effect', which gives to those that already have, is a consequence of increasing returns to scale in the economics of scientific research and technological innovation.[1] It poses a major challenge to the building of endogenous science and technology capabilities, and also highlights the importance of international cooperation to assist developing countries in meeting this challenge.

All this suggests that the science and technology capabilities, as well as the information and communications technological infrastructure, of most developing countries are far too limited to deal adequately with the challenges they face at the beginning of the 21st century. In many cases they also lack the capacity to effectively select, absorb, adapt and use imported knowledge and technologies, and the capacity for identifying and selectively upgrading traditional knowledge and techniques.

Severe resource constraints and growing social demands force developing country leaders to make difficult decisions between alleviating poverty in the short term and building capacities to generate and utilize knowledge in the medium and long term – which would later help to reduce poverty to a much larger extent. The metaphor of a starving farmer eating the seed needed to plant next year's crop comes to mind when confronting such painful choices.

4.2   DISPARITIES BETWEEN DEVELOPING COUNTRIES: A SCIENCE AND TECHNOLOGY (S&T) CAPACITY INDEX

While the knowledge divide between developed and developing countries is the most noticeable feature of the contemporary knowledge and innovation scene, disparities between developing countries are also very large. As a consequence, strategies and policies to build endogenous science and technology capabilities have to be tailored to their specific situations. However, it is possible to identify general categories to group countries with similar knowledge, technology and innovation capabilities into a few categories to orient the design of such strategies and policies.

The conceptual framework advanced in Chapter 1 (Figure 1.1) suggests a way of constructing an index that combines the capacities to conduct scientific research, to generate science-based technologies, and to incorporate the results of research and technological development into production through innovation. Ideally, the construction of an index to measure the degree to which a country has built an endogenous science and technology capacity should reflect the intensity of interactions between knowledge, technology and production in the process of innovation. However, measuring the intensity of these interactions is a most difficult task, feasible only through detailed case studies that produce data that are not amenable to statistical aggregation. Moreover, as there are no indicators of the level of traditional knowledge, technology and production capabilities, it is impossible to build this very important aspect into the design of the index. For these reasons, rather than attempting to construct a broad 'Knowledge and Innovation Capacity Index', a narrower 'Science and Technology (S&T) Capacity Index' has been designed.

Box 4.1 describes the components and the method of calculation for the S&T Capacity Index, which allows us to place countries along the spectrum of science and technology capabilities and to group them in reasonably homogeneous categories. The idea has been to select and combine individual indicators that represent the level of domestic capacities in scientific research, technological development and the incorporation of new technologies

BOX 4.1   THE SCIENCE AND TECHNOLOGY (S&T) CAPACITY INDEX

Components of the Index. The components of the science and technology capacity index are derived from the conceptual model proposed in Chapter 1. The indicators of internal capacity and of external linkages for science, technology and production are:

SCIENCE	TECHNOLOGY	PRODUCTION
Internal capacity: Expenditures in research and development/GDP	Number of scientists and engineers per million people	Gross product of knowledge intensive production sectors/GDP[1]
External linkages: Number of scientific publications (in logarithms)[4]	Number of patent applications filed by residents and non-residents (in logarithms)[2] [4]	Infrastructure, communications and technology index[3]

The following observations are in order about some of the indicators:

(1)   Due to lack of data, the indicator actually used as a proxy was 'high-technology exports as a percentage of total exports'.

(2)   Although other authors use the number of US patents by country of origin as a proxy measure of external linkages in the case of technology capacity, this indicator may be strongly biased in favor of industrialized countries (88 per cent of all patents registered in the US originate from the United States, Japan and three countries of the European Union). For this reason we prefer to use the total number of patent applications. In addition, the considerable administrative costs of obtaining a US patent may discourage some inventors from developing countries from applying for US patents.

(3) The index of infrastructure, communications and technology is a composite indicator that includes numbers of television sets, fax machines, personal computers, internet hosts and mobile phones available in a given country. This indicator was elaborated by Francisco Rodríguez and Ernest J. Wilson, *Are poor countries losing the information revolution?* Infodev Working Paper, available at http://www.worldbank.org/infodev.

(4) These two indicators are specified in logarithms to prevent the very large number of publications and patents of the United States from distorting the results during the normalization process.

Calculation of the Index. The S&T Capacity Index is the simple average of the internal and external indexes, as follows:

S&T Capacity Index = (Internal capacity$_i$ + External linkages$_i$)/2

Where i = country 1, 2, 3, ..., n

To normalize the value of each country indicator, the six indicators that make up both indices were calculated in the following way:

$$I_{ij} = \frac{X_{ij} - min X_j}{max X_j - min X_j} \quad i = 1,...,85 \quad j = 1,...,6$$

Where I = Value of the indicator
i = Country (85 countries in total)
j = Indicator (six in total, see table above)
X_{ij} = Value of the country indicator
$min X_j$ = Minimum value of the indicator j
$max X_j$ = Maximum value of the indicator j

into production, and also the extent of the linkages between these and their international counterparts. The three indicators of internal capacity are normalized and averaged in a simple manner, the same is done for the three indicators of external linkages, and the S&T Capacity Index is calculated as the simple average of these two averages. While it would be possible to assign weights to each of the indicators, so as to reflect the relative importance of each component of internal capacity and of external linkages, this has not been done in this exercise.[2]

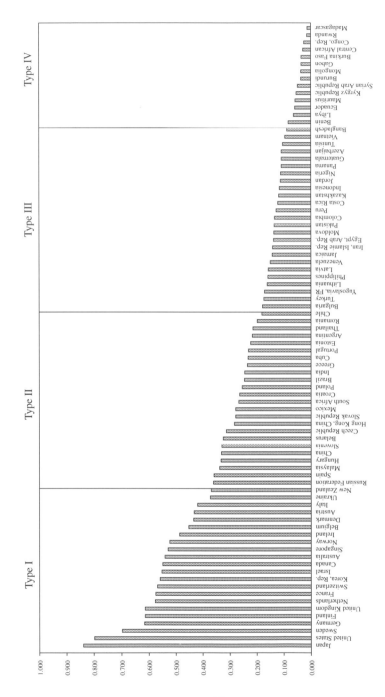

Figure 4.1   Ranking of countries according to their Science and Technology (S&T) Capacity Index

Figure 4.1 shows the results of the calculation of the S&T Capacity Index for the 85 countries with available data. The values of the index vary over a wide range, but suggest that there are four distinct groups of countries as follows:

Type I. These countries have well developed endogenous scientific and technological capacities, have advanced research and innovation capacities that continuously renew their stock of knowledge and their production facilities, their national systems of innovation operate effectively, and government policies support the generation, acquisition and utilization of knowledge. Their science and technology linkages with other countries are very strong, and they are the world's leaders in the trade of technology intensive goods.

Type II. These countries have moderate levels of endogenous scientific and technological capacities, usually focused on the dynamic sectors of their economies. Even though most of them have a reasonably well-developed stock of human resources, they have not been able to create a broad science and technology research base that is effectively linked to production. They are actively engaged in scientific and technological exchanges with other countries, and usually focus on how to take advantage of the stock of knowledge available in Type I countries.

Type III. These countries are still in the early stages of establishing modern production systems. They have a rather limited stock of highly qualified human resources, and incipient scientific research, technological development and innovation capacities. Many have a few enclaves of modern production activities (usually associated with foreign investment) that coexist with large segments of production activities based on traditional and conventional technologies, most of which are not able to compete in world markets. They face information, institutional and financial problems, and their linkages with the external sources of knowledge and technology are weak and sporadic.

Type IV. These countries have practically no significant scientific research, technological development or innovation capacities, and also have a very limited human resources base. Apart from the extraction of natural resources or the provision of some services, which take place in isolated enclaves, they generally use traditional and conventional technologies, which operate at low levels of productivity and efficiency. Linkages with the world scientific and technological community are extremely limited and in some cases non-existent.

Table 4.2   Average values of the indicators and of the Science and Technology (S&T) Capacity Index by group of countries

| | Internal Capacity | | | External linkages | | | |
Type of country	Number of scientists and engineers	R&D expenditures/ GDP	Exports of high-technology sectors/total exports	Scientific publications	Number of patent applications filed	Infrastructure, communications and technology index	S&T Capacity Index
Type I	0.438	0.610	0.438	0.353	0.225	0.547	0.435
Type II	0.203	0.220	0.229	0.074	0.070	0.164	0.158
Type III	0.063	0.123	0.101	0.010	0.019	0.055	0.062
Type IV	0.026	0.034	0.005	0.002	0.016	0.024	0.017

Source: Sagasti and Prada (2000).

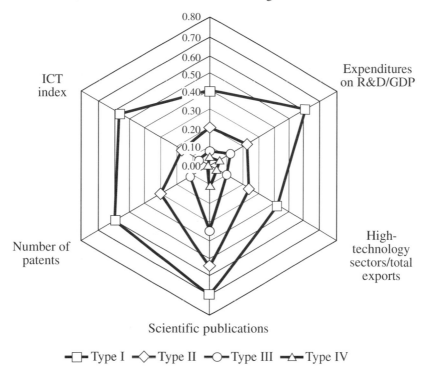

Number of scientists and engineers

ICT index

Expenditures on R&D/GDP

Number of patents

High-technology sectors/total exports

Scientific publications

—□— Type I   —◇— Type II   —○— Type III   —△— Type IV

Note: ICT index refers to the infrastructure and communication index compiled by the World Bank (see Box 4.1).

Source: Sagasti and Prada (2000).

Figure 4.2   Typology of countries according to the value of the indicators in the Science and Technology (S&T) Capacity Index

Table 4.2 and Figure 4.2 show the average values of the indicators comprising the S&T Capacity Index for each of these four categories of countries. There is large difference between the average values of Type I countries, which have acquired an endogenous scientific and technological base, and those of Type II, III and IV countries that still lack it, although to differing degrees, as is also clearly shown in Figure 4.3. This suggests the presence of an increasing returns to scale phenomenon, in which countries that already have endogenous technology capabilities are able to continue on developing such capacities at a greater rate than those that have not been able to do so.[3]

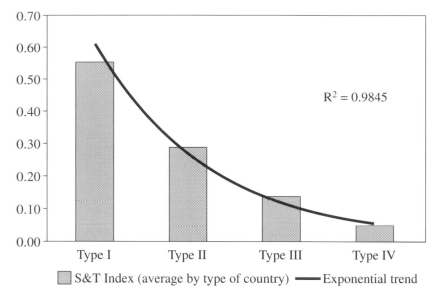

Source: Sagasti and Prada (2000).

*Figure 4.3   Science and Technology (S&T) Capacity Index: averages for
             each category*

There have been other exercises aimed at developing indexes of science
and technology capabilities, including those conducted by the United Nations Industrial Development Organization (UNIDO, 2002), Wagner et al.
(2001), the United Nations Development Programme (UNDP, 2001), and
by the International Council for Science Policy in a report prepared for the
United Nations Education, Science and Culture Organization (UNESCO,
1990). Table 4.3 compares the various components of these other indexes.
Even though these exercises are not based on an underlying conceptual
framework such as the one proposed in Chapter 2 of this book, they lead to
similar results with regards to groups of countries. Appendix 1 contains a
detailed comparison of the categories used in these five classification schemes
and of the place occupied by countries in each of them. In addition, UNIDO's
Industrial Development Report 2002/2003 has developed a composite index to benchmark industrial performance and rank 86 countries according
to it, although the report does not offer a classification scheme similar to
the other ones analyzed in this section. The variables used to construct
UNIDO's benchmarking index are also indicated in Appendix 1.

Table 4.3 Comparison between the components of four indexes of science and technology capabilities

Index	Dimension and indicators	Index	Dimension and indicators
Science and Technology (S&T) Capacity Index	*Science* • Number of scientists and engineers • Scientific publications *Technology* • Expenditures on R&D/GDP • Number cf patent applications filed *Production* • Exports of high-technology sectors/total exports • Infrastructure, communications and technology index	RAND	*Infrastructure* • Gross national product (GNP) per capita *Human resources available for S&T activities* • Number of scientists and engineers per million people *S&T outputs* • Number of S&T journal articles and patents produced by citizens • Number of patents filed through the US Patent and Trademark Office (USPTO) and the European Patent Office (EPO). *Input into S&T* • Percentage of GNP spent on R&D *External knowledge sources* • Number of the nation's students studying in the United States adjusted for those who chose not to return home at the conclusion of their studies

71

Table 4.3 continued

Index	Dimension and indicators	Index	Dimension and indicators
Technology Achievement Index (TAI)	*Creation of technology* • Patents granted per capita • Receipts of royalty and license fees from abroad per capita *Diffusion of recent innovations* • Internet hosts per capita • High- and medium-technology exports as a share of all exports *Diffusion of old innovations* • Logarithm of telephones per capita (mainline and cellular combined) • Logarithm of electricity consumption per capita *Human skills* • Mean years of schooling • Gross enrolment ratio at tertiary level in science, mathematics and engineering	UNESCO	*The distribution of overall human resources* • Distribution of countries according to population *The distribution of income levels* • GDP per capita • % of manufactured products exports from total national exports and total developing countries manufactured exports. *Research and development intensity* • R&D share of the GNP • Scientists and engineers in the population • R&D personnel in higher education per 1000 population *Accomplishments in S&T education* • Number of potential scientists and engineers • Number of R&D scientists per million population • Number of third-level students per 100 000 inhabitants. • R&D personnel in industry *An overall typology of S&T capabilities* • 'Scoreboard' according to groupings achieved by countries in each case

Source: Sagasti and Prada (2000).

The S&T Capacity Index uses as components indicators of science, technology and production activities, and thus focuses exclusively on the capacity to generate and utilize knowledge, and does not consider any indicator of economic development or general welfare of the population. Nevertheless, there is a high correlation between the S&T Capacity Index and the Human Development Index (HDI) calculated by UNDP, which includes income per capita, life expectancy and years of schooling. Figure 4.4 shows clearly that Type I countries belong to the category of high HDI, Type II and III belong to the medium HDI group, while Type IV coincides with the category of countries with low HDI.[4]

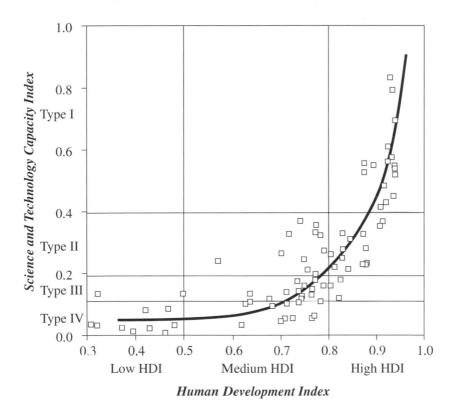

Source: Sagasti and Prada (2000).

Figure 4.4   The Human Development Index (HDI) and the Science and Technology (S&T) Capacity Index

NOTES

1. This term derives from St Matthew's account of the 'Parable of the talents' in which Jesus Christ rewards an industrious man who received more money and used it well, in contrast to two others who were given less and failed to make proper use of the amounts they received.
2. All the tables, figures and graphs in this section have been taken from Sagasti and Prada (2000).
3. The usual caveats that apply to the use of indicators in general, such as lack or poor quality of data and inconsistent use of definitions, apply when measuring such a complex set of capabilities included in the S&T Capacity Index. In addition, there are some limitations specific to these indicators. First, the use of 'high-technology exports as a percentage of total exports' as a proxy for 'gross product of knowledge intensive production sectors as a percentage of GDP' is problematic. Exports do not necessarily denote internal capacity, especially in countries with high foreign direct investment. Second, the lack and poor quality of data introduce distortions in the indicators for type III and IV countries, and the value of some indicators might be grossly overestimated or underestimated. In order to keep the consistency of the series for each indicator, instead of combining data from different sources to increase the number of countries in some of the series we have used data from a single source, which is the UNESCO World Science Report.
4. The Human Development Index data was obtained from the UNDP website http://www.undp. org/hdro/hdro.html.

5. Strategies and policies for building an endogenous science and technology base

The preceding chapters have made explicit the Sisyphean challenge faced by developing countries in mobilizing knowledge for development. The obstacles that must be surmounted in responding adequately to it suggest the need for well-thought-out strategies and for effective policy instruments, so as to make the best possible use of scarce resources and limited opportunities. However, even the best efforts by developing countries are unlikely to succeed in an adverse global context. Without a positive attitude and the active engagement of the global scientific and technological community, of international institutions and government agencies in developed countries, and of private sector firms, universities and research centers that control the access to knowledge and technology, it will be nearly impossible for developing countries to bridge the knowledge divide and to build endogenous science and technology capabilities. For this reason, international cooperation plays a special role in meeting this challenge.

5.1 THE CONTEXT FOR MOBILIZING KNOWLEDGE AND INNOVATION FOR DEVELOPMENT

Efforts to mobilize knowledge and innovation to improve the human condition will take place in the context of a turbulent, segmented and uneven globalization process. At the beginning of the 21st century, the accelerated expansion of production and service activities throughout the world, the rapid growth of international trade and the massive exchanges of information that can be accessed anywhere in the planet, coexist with the concentration of such 'global' activities in certain countries, regions, cities and even neighborhoods, and a large proportion of these 'globalized' exchanges take place within a few hundred transnational corporations.

The simultaneous integration and exclusion of countries, regions – as well as of peoples within countries – are two intertwining aspects of the many faceted paradoxical processes of globalization and fragmentation under way in our turbulent period of history, a time that is witnessing the emergence of a *fractured global order*. This is an order that is global but not integrated, which puts us in contact with one another but at the same time preserves and creates deep divisions between countries and between peoples in these countries, and an order which benefits a small part of humanity and segregates the vast majority of the world's population.

The emergence of this fractured global order has old historical roots. As pointed out in Chapter 2, the fissures that characterized the globalization process now under way began to appear in the 15th and 16th centuries, with the worldwide expansion of Western Europe. Yet, the swift and profound upheavals of the last half of the 20th century have created a radically new context for human evolution. To a very large extent, this is because advances in science and technology – closely associated with the transformation of knowledge generation activities, the changes in the technological base and the modifications of production activities (Chapter 3) – have wrought profound changes in the way human beings interact, in our conceptions of human nature and in the way we visualize the future evolution of humanity.

Ambiguities, contradictions and inconsistencies, which generate confusion and uncertainty, accompany this uneven process of globalization and fragmentation. The various forces – political, security, economic, financial, social, environmental, cultural, governance, religious, scientific and technological – that interact to produce the fractured global order do not all pull in the same direction. They may generate positive or negative results depending on the structure of power relations of those affected by them, and also on the capacity to design and put into practice strategies to take advantage of opportunities and to limit undesirable effects. Considered alone, any one of these forces of change has important consequences for the future of developing countries and, indeed, for the whole planet. Taken together, they represent an epochal change, a fundamental shift in the international frame of reference for efforts to achieve prosperity and well-being, which demands a fundamental reappraisal of how the emerging international context shapes options for developing countries.

The fractured global order gives rise to a series of demands which require strategic responses from governments, businesses and civil society organizations in developing countries. The emergence of *new international security concerns* – ethnic and religious conflicts, chemical and bacteriological warfare, terrorism, proliferation of nuclear weapons, organized crime, drug trafficking and environmental disputes – demands new arrangements for international and regional security, as well as new national defense doctrines. This became evident after the 11 September 2001 terrorist attacks on the World Trade Center in New York and the Pentagon in Washington.

Growing *economic and financial interdependence*, together with changes in international economic relations, demand new strategies for the insertion of economies and businesses in an increasingly integrated, competitive and volatile international scene, in which financial globalization plays a leading role.

Social conditions and persistent inequalities pose an enormous challenge to the maintenance of social cohesion. Demographic imbalances between rich and poor countries; rapid growth in the demand for food, health, education, housing, drinking water and sewerage services in the developing world; widespread poverty associated with economic, political and social exclusion; and unemployment and underemployment, which affect rich countries as well as poor, all require imaginative and practical responses both at the international, national and local levels. Similarly, the significant changes which have occurred in gender relations, primarily as a result of the ability women have acquired to regulate more easily their own fertility, have great importance for the world of work and home: they demand a new perspective on the conventional division of responsibilities between men and women, both in the workplace and in the upbringing of children.

Awareness of the imperative of *environmental protection and the sustainable use of natural resources*, associated with the appearance of environmental problems of a regional and global nature, demands responses to ensure that economic growth, widespread poverty and unsustainable consumption patterns do not limit the opportunities of future generations. The scale and intensity of human activity means that we cannot now blindly trust in the automatic regenerative capacity of ecosystems, but must consciously devise environmentally friendly ways of going about our business on an increasingly fragile planet.

Religious, ethical and cultural factors in the conduct of government and business affairs add fresh demands to an already overcrowded public agenda. They bring to the fore issues such as religious tolerance, respect for human rights, ethical behavior, and highlight the tensions between pressures towards cultural homogeneity and the affirmation of cultural identity. The *spread of democratic practices* and the collapse of one-party totalitarian systems in Eastern Europe and the former Soviet Union have wrought significant changes in the institutional structures of states and governments, and brought to our attention the importance of social capital and institutions in political and economic performance.

In addition, *advances in science, technology and innovation* are both a cause and a consequence of all the other changes in the forces that are shaping the emerging fractured global order, as described in Chapters 2 and 3 of this book.

It should be kept in mind that only certain sectors of the global economy, including financial services, manufactured products with a high technological content, mass media and telecommunications, have expanded their activities worldwide. As highlighted in Chapter 3, section 3.5, a large proportion of production and service activities remain firmly anchored in their local settings. This is the case of many agricultural activities, small manufacturing, crafts and a whole range of services whose geographical reach is limited, and also of practically all activities linked to subsistence economies. It is difficult to estimate what percentage of the world's population remains outside the global circuits of production, commerce, finance and consumption, but it is likely that a significant proportion of those who live in poor countries do not participate and are little affected by them.

Nobody is directing in any conscious or deliberate manner the processes leading to a fractured global order. There is no overall coordinator who takes decisions on the course of the contradictory processes of globalization and fragmentation – no one is 'in charge' of the turbulent processes that are creating a few winners and many losers. Their diverse components function in accordance to their own logic and the logics of the interactions between them. However, this does not mean that the processes leading to a fractured global order lack a general direction which – for the time being – is rooted in the pro-market and anti-state ideological stance prevalent at the end of the 20th century, although it is now shifting to a more balanced perspective of the role of the state, the market and civil society in the process of development.

The fractured global order, with all its paradoxes and ambiguities, constitutes the stage on which developing countries will face the Sisyphean challenge of building endogenous science and technology capabilities. An adequate appreciation of its main features and implications is essential for developing countries to improve their chances of meeting this challenge.

5.2   THE EXPERIENCE WITH SCIENCE AND TECHNOLOGY POLICIES IN THE DEVELOPING COUNTRIES

As the growing importance of science and technology began to be recognized during the second half of the 20th century, several countries designed and put into practice strategies and policies to build scientific and technological capabilities. These policies responded to their specific situations, historical backgrounds and to the foresight of their political, business and academic leaders, which conditioned their content and success to a very large extent. The rather long time required to build and consolidate knowledge, technology and innovation capacities ensures that the inertia of past interventions and outcomes influences the range of options available to policy- and decision-makers at any given time. In particular, the coverage and quality of education – especially tertiary education in the physical, biological and engineering sciences – exerts a determining influence on what can be achieved in scientific research, technological development and innovation.

The values of the Scientific and Technological Capacity Index and the typology put forward in Chapter 4, Section 4.2, describe the result of country strategies and policies put into practice during several decades. For example, the Republic of Korea is the only country in the Type I category which started nearly five decades ago as a very poor country, with practically no domestic knowledge and innovation capabilities. Massive investments in education science and technology allowed South Korea to catch up with the more advanced countries of the West in just a few decades. Also, starting from relatively low levels, Israel and to a lesser extent Ireland may be said to have moved relatively fast in the acquisition of science and technology capabilities. In contrast, the countries placed in the Type IV category have made little or no effort to systematically build their science and technology capacities, largely because of a host of political and economic limitations that have put and have kept them at a disadvantage. The Sisyphus syndrome, whereby hard-won science and technology capacities are lost because of the inability to sustain efforts, can be clearly observed in many developing countries during the past five decades, and more recently in the countries of Eastern Europe and the former Soviet Union.

The study, design and execution of science and technology policies, as we understand them now, began in the period immediately after World War II, a few years after this field was defined and delimited in the seminal work of J.D. Bernal, *The Social Function of Science*.[1] At that time governments in industrialized nations started to emphasize the application of science to peaceful uses, following the success with which it had been used during the war. Science and technology policy studies and practice evolved through several phases, marking a gradual transition from concerns centered around the growth of scientific research in the 1950s, towards preoccupations with technological innovation and competitiveness in the following decades. In parallel, a number of science and technology policy research programs were established in Europe and the United States, and over a period of three decades these programs created a well-established field of study and practice. A similar evolution took place in a few developing countries – India, Brazil, Egypt, South Korea and Mexico – where these studies were often encouraged and supported by international institutions, including the United Nations Educational, Scientific and Cultural Organization (UNESCO), the United Nations Trade and Development Conference (UNCTAD), the Organization of American States (OAS) and the Canadian International Development Research Centre (IDRC).

Perceptions of the role of science and technology in development evolved from a rather optimistic view in the 1950s and 1960s, to a more skeptical

perspective in the 1980s and 1990s. Along the way, valuable experience –
both positive and negative – was accumulated regarding how to design and
implement strategies and policies to acquire knowledge and innovation capacities.

Five partially overlapping phases can be identified in the evolution of
science and technology policies for development, based primarily on what
happened in those regions and countries that attempted to build capabilities
in this field: Latin America, several countries in South and South-East Asia,
and a few countries in Africa and the Middle East. First, there was a *science
push* phase, which extended from the early 1950s to the mid-1960s. The
design of science and technology policies during this phase was shaped by
the 'linear innovation model' perspective, in which scientific research led
directly to technological innovation, which, in turn, improved productivity
and economic growth. Therefore, the main task was to boost the scientific
capacity to produce discoveries and inventions. This approach led to a surge
of support for the creation of scientific research facilities in universities and
public institutions. Many developing countries created national research councils at this stage, which were given the task of promoting and financing
scientific research.

Second, there was a *technology transfer and systems analysis* phase that
began in the late 1960s and lasted through the 1970s. Technology transfers
and the choice of appropriate technologies were the main concerns in this
phase. Direct foreign investment, particularly by transnational corporations,
played an important role in relocating some technologically mature industries
in developing countries. While these investments were viewed in a positive
light because of their potential impact on industrial transformation, employment generation and productivity improvements, the policies used to attract
direct foreign investment backfired in many developing countries. High tariff
barriers for consumer and light durable goods, coupled with low tariffs for
capital goods and intermediate products and with generous tax incentives,
succeeded in attracting transnational corporations to countries with relatively
large internal markets. However, they also led to external accounts imbalances due to poor export performance, increases in machinery and materials
imports, profit remittances and hefty management and technology licensing
fees. The response was to establish government agencies to regulate foreign
direct investment, technology license agreements and to provide information
about technological options to domestic firms. These were accompanied by
efforts to promote the use of 'appropriate technologies', defined as those
requiring less capital investments and skilled labor, those better suited to
domestic consumer tastes and those that made use of local natural resources.

In the mid to late 1970s, technology transfer concerns were superseded
by attempts to apply a 'systems approach' to the design and implementation

of science and technology policies. The limited success of what were seen as narrowly focused efforts justified the adoption of comprehensive approaches to science and technology capacity-building. The greater availability of empirical studies of technological development, together with evaluations of the impact of science and technology policies, provided a more informed basis for policy design. Yet these policies were still primarily centered on how to improve the performance of government agencies, universities and public research institutions. The consolidation of technological and innovation capacities in the private sector did not figure prominently as a policy concern, and firms remained largely isolated from domestic scientific research and technological development institutions. At this time, many 'national research councils' were transformed into 'national science and technology councils', which considerably increased their scope in comparison with the focus on research and development that dominated the in previous phase.

Third, a *science and technology policy implementation phase* began in the mid-1970s and extended through the mid-1980s. Priority was given to policies to promote technological change in manufacturing, agriculture, mining and other priority sectors, and also to improve the technological capacity of private and state-owned firms. Special funds to support innovation were established, fiscal incentives for research and development were created, and information, quality control and training programs were launched to assist enterprises. One of the core concerns in this phase was assessing the impact of science and technology policies on the behavior of economic agents and of science and technology institutions. This led to a number of comparative studies on the design and implementation of technology policies, on the impact of these policies on the behavior of production units, and on the difference between implicit and explicit science and technology policies, all of which were supposed to help in the identification of more effective science and technology policy instruments.[2]

The fourth phase, which prevailed during most of the 1980s and stretched into the early 1990s, could be labeled as that of *disregard for science and technology policies and emphasis on the free play of market forces*. The economic crises in Latin America, Sub-Saharan Africa, and in some countries of South Asia and Asia-Pacific, led to drastic reductions in government budgets and in public allocations for science and technology. Macroeconomic disequilibria – high inflation, exchange rate misalignment, trade and fiscal deficits – became common in developing countries, at the same time that growing external debt payments exerted pressures on foreign exchange earnings and fiscal accounts. As a response, international financial institutions designed and pressed for economic policy reforms – trade and financial liberalization, privatization, deregulation, tax reform and fiscal discipline, among others – which were codified in what was labeled as the 'Washington Consensus' in the late 1980s.

In this context, most firms halted long-term investments and relegated technology concerns to a second or third plane. Maintaining financial health in an unstable economic environment became the overriding concern of managers and entrepreneurs, while operational, technical and human resource issues became much less important. The few state-owned firms that had played a leading role in technology curtailed their research and development activities, and many professionals in technology research, development and management left these firms and emigrated. During this phase, many developing countries experienced the loss of science, technology and innovation capabilities that had taken substantive efforts and a long time to build.

There is a substantive overlap between the fourth phase in the design and implementation of science and technology policies, and the current phase of *competitiveness and innovation systems*, which emerged in the mid-1990s. Economic policy reforms led to price, exchange rate and fiscal stability, but did not generate sustained growth or improved social equity. Firms that survived the tough process of commercial and financial liberalization increased their efficiency and became more competitive, but a large number of enterprises that catered for domestic markets disappeared together with their technological and innovation capacities. In addition, the attainment of fiscal stability and the redirection of public expenditures towards social support programs to ameliorate the impact of adjustment policies led, in an indirect way, to reductions in public budget resources for science and technology.

The East Asian financial crisis of 1997–99 offers an interesting contrast in the way developing regions responded to severe downturns in their rates of economic growth. When output declined significantly in the Republic of Korea, Thailand, Malaysia, Indonesia and the Philippines, these countries were forced to reduce significantly public expenditures. Yet, several of them – most notably Korea and Malaysia – protected their investments in science and technology capabilities by introducing modest budget cuts and by encouraging the private sector to maintain the level of their research and development expenditures. These actions confirmed the centrality assigned by these countries to the link between science and technology capabilities and economic growth, and may partly explain why, once the financial crisis subsided, they were able to resume their high rates of economic and export growth. To a significant extent these two countries had the advantage of possessing a vigorous and forward-looking export-orientated domestic private sector, and of not following the advice of the international financial institutions in the way they dealt with the crisis. This is in sharp contrast with what happened in Latin America a decade earlier and during the crises of the 1990s, where capital flight, a reduction on direct foreign investment and severe cuts in public expenditures had a negative impact on their science and technology capabilities and, as indicated earlier, destroyed capacities that had been laboriously acquired during more than two decades.

A reappraisal of the policies contained in the 'Washington Consensus' in the late 1990s identified the need for a 'second generation' of policy reforms focusing on institutional development, the rule of law, accountability and openness in government, and on a better balance between state intervention, market forces and civil society participation. The need to penetrate foreign markets led to initiatives to improve competitiveness, and to a renewed interest in science and technology policies. The emphasis shifted towards strengthening technology and innovation capacities in firms, with research facilities and technology institutes playing a supporting role in the quest for competitiveness. The role of science and technology councils became fuzzier and less important, especially as new technical assistance, quality control, market information, certification and financing programs outside their purview were launched to support innovation. These were complemented with measures to encourage commercial spin-offs from university and research institutes, the creation of technology parks to attract high technology foreign investment, and the consolidation of clusters of small and medium-size enterprises around large modern firms to promote technology diffusion. Some of these measures had been tried before with mixed success, but they were now seen as components of a comprehensive approach to innovation and competitiveness.

The concept of 'national innovation systems' provided a framework to view and articulate science and technology policies in this phase. Similar to what the systems approach advocated in the late 1970s, this concept emphasizes the roles played by a wide variety of capable and strongly interacting agents to engender innovation. However, it does so in the setting of competitive markets that extend beyond national boundaries, while focusing more sharply on the role of enterprises and stressing the need for monitoring, evaluation and continuous adjustment of government policies. The acquisition and effective utilization of knowledge in production and service activities is considered a key source of competitive advantage, and the activities of public and private universities, research institutes, consulting firms and other agents involved in the generation and transmission of knowledge must feed innovation and technological learning. With a long-term perspective, this amounts to tightly binding science, technology and production, which would gradually lead to the creation of an endogenous science and technology base. However, in the short and medium term, an innovation system will rely more on imported sources of knowledge and technology, while scientific and technological research capabilities are built and consolidated.

Although not all developing countries experienced these five phases at the same time and in the same sequence, on the whole they show the main science and technology policy trends during the past 50 years. Yet, in spite of their evolution, and with a very few notable exceptions, the impact of these policies has been rather limited. In most developing countries, scientific research, technology development and innovation capacities remained incipient and isolated from each other. The rather low participation of developing countries in the world's scientific and technological effort did not improve in any significant way during the past half century. Building endogenous science and technology capacities has proven to be a most difficult task in the vast majority of developing countries. Nevertheless, many useful lessons have been learned and can be taken advantage of in the Sisyphean task of mobilizing knowledge and innovation to improve the human condition.

5.3   AN APPROACH TO STRATEGY AND POLICY DESIGN

The preoccupation with the design and implementation of national development strategies re-emerged in the mid-1990s, as the competitiveness and innovation phase of science and technology policies began to take shape. This followed more than a decade of dominance of ideas and policies based on the free play of market forces as the preferred path to the improvement of living standards in developing countries, during which influential academic researchers, opinion leaders and senior officials in international organizations sought to reduce the role played by the state in the economies of developing countries. To this end they promoted liberalization, deregulation and privatization policies, often without the necessary institutional prerequisites in place (regulating agencies, accountability procedures, government transparency and openness). The undesirable consequences of this approach – growing inequalities between and within countries, increases in the number of poor people, widespread exclusion, and corruption of senior government officials, among others – became evident during the 1990s, and a more balanced perspective on the role of market forces, state intervention and civil society participation has begun to emerge. This happened together with the transition from the fourth phase of science and technology policies, which relied on market forces, to the current phase, which emphasizes competitiveness and the role of national innovation systems.

The return of strategy to center stage in development thinking and practice coincided with a growing interest in the role played by knowledge in development, and also with advances in strategic planning in complex organizations, which provided methodological tools to organize comprehensive and participative planning processes. The emergence of the knowledge society, the knowledge explosion and its manifestations, and the visibility of the knowledge divide made it necessary to explicitly incorporate science, technology and innovation – as well as the recovery of traditional knowledge and techniques – into the design of development strategies.

However, in most developing countries there is not as yet widespread awareness and understanding of the importance of science and technology in the contemporary world, nor an acceptance that short-term sacrifices must be made to build the capacities to generate and utilize knowledge. A first task is to raise social consciousness about the critical role that knowledge plays in development, and to persuade political, grass roots, community, business and civil society leaders that science, technology and innovation are essential to improve living standards. It is also necessary to call their attention to the huge and growing disparities in the capacity to generate and utilize knowledge, which are at the root of the asymmetries in power relations between governments and firms in developed and in developing countries, and which considerably limit the room for maneuver in the design and implementation of development strategies.

There are several principles to guide the design and implementation of strategies to create and acquire endogenous science and technology capabilities. These have emerged out of the experience, both positive and negative, of many developing countries in the last five decades.

The first principle is that *strategies and policies for establishing an endogenous science and technology base must be fully incorporated into the design of a comprehensive development strategy for the country.* Isolated attempts at creating pockets of science, technology and innovation capabilities without strong linkages to broader development objectives, and to the means for achieving them, are unsustainable in the long run. Conversely, development strategies that do not envisage a major role for science, technology and innovation are likely to fail in the knowledge society of the 21st century. The often heroic efforts of science and technology researchers and policy-makers in developing countries are futile in the face of indifference, neglect and even hostility by political, government and business leaders. The few developing countries that have made spectacular economic and social gains during the last few decades are precisely those that adopted development strategies that envisaged a key role for science and technology. Because the social and private rates of return to investments in scientific research, technological development and innovation differ widely, this requires a strong public sector presence, at least in the initial stages of building an endogenous science and technology base. Those activities are characterized by strong externalities that prevent private agents from reaping the full benefit of their efforts. In many of its forms, knowledge is clearly a 'public good', which many people can take advantage of without diminishing its usefulness to others.[3] As Thomas Jefferson put it 'he who receives an idea from me receives [it] without lessening [me], as he who lights his [candle] at mine receives light without darkening me'.

The second principle acknowledges that *the cumulative process of building endogenous science and technology capabilities requires continuous and sustained efforts over a long time.* There are many prerequisites for success in this enterprise – macroeconomic stability, an educated human resource base, well-functioning institutions, an active research community, and open-minded and innovative entrepreneurs, among others – and these are not acquired overnight. History counts and the results of previous efforts condition the options available to policy- and decision-makers. Institutions take a long time to build and there is no substitute for the steady evolution of practices and habits of interaction that create a favorable environment for science and technology. Nevertheless, while maintaining a steady course in the long-term process of building science and technology capabilities, there must also be a readiness to take advantage of unexpected short-term opportunities (discovery of natural resources, economic windfalls, availability of new technologies, geopolitical shifts). Occasionally, there may emerge possibilities for 'leapfrogging' into more advanced technological stages, but leapfrogging requires 'technological legs' that take time to grow. Persistence must be balanced with flexibility in the process of building an endogenous science and technology base.[4] A corollary of this principle is the readiness to accept failure, for it is most improbable that each and every policy intervention will be successful during the decade or two that would be required, in the best possible circumstances, to create an adequate level of scientific research, technological development and innovation capabilities.

The third principle is derived from the difficult economic situation and the scarcity of resources that beset most developing countries. *The process of building endogenous science and technology capabilities must be highly selective, but without losing sight of unusual opportunities that may emerge.* This argues for focusing efforts on a few clearly identified areas of science, technology and production, while leaving space and a modest amount of resources to support non-priority but potentially useful initiatives. Adhering to this principle requires a willingness to make choices in the face of uncertainty (about technological advances, the international context, institutional performance, the behavior of researchers and entrepreneurs), fully acknowledging the long-term consequences of such difficult decisions. The selection process locks in resources for a decade or more in the chosen areas and their upstream and downstream linkages, which puts a premium on using the best available information and decision making procedures.

The fourth principle emphasizes the integrative nature of the process of building an endogenous science and technology base, where *science, technology and production, together with traditional knowledge and techniques, must all be fully integrated.* Within the chosen priority areas, measures to develop scientific research, technological development and innovation capacities, as well as to promote their interactions, must be viewed as a coherent whole and adopted in a logical sequence to increase the likelihood of success. It is not enough to build excellent scientific research capacities, expecting they will automatically lead to technological development; nor it is sufficient to import advanced technologies to improve production, assuming that they will trickle down and enrich technological capabilities. This underscores the importance of thinking about 'knowledge and technology delivery systems' that can foster and sustain innovation. As the innovation process has acquired a more systemic character, and as the age of analysis yields to the age synthesis in technology development, engineering skills and capabilities have become the glue that holds together the various knowledge, technology and production components. Therefore, building engineering schools and creating technology management programs are among the high-priority tasks in the acquisition of endogenous science and technology capabilities.

The fifth principle is related to the global character of modern science and technology: *the international dimension must be explicitly considered in the design of strategies to build an endogenous science and technology base.* This implies encouraging cooperation in scientific research, securing access to the sources of technology, promoting trade in knowledge-intensive goods and services, creating conditions to attract foreign investment that brings technology to the country, fostering the exchange of highly trained personnel, making use of graduate fellowship programs, and harmonizing policies and international agreements that regulate the global flow of knowledge and technology. Putting in practice this principle requires close coordination between policy-makers in charge of science and technology on the one side, and those responsible for international trade, foreign investment, higher education, selected economic sectors and diplomacy on the other. The international negotiations agenda of developing countries should include the expansion and better coordination of cooperation initiatives to support their science and technology efforts, particularly in view of the limited number and dispersion of existing international organizations, programs, mechanisms and facilities supporting science and technology in developing countries.

The sixth principle emphasizes the importance of *adopting a learning stance in the process of building an endogenous science and technology base.* The effectiveness and efficiency of policy instruments should be continuously monitored and evaluated, but allowing time for them to influence the behavior of the variety of agents engaged in the generation, acquisition, dissemination and utilization of knowledge. As domestic and international conditions change rapidly, policies, policy instruments and the procedures to put them in practice are likely to require adjustments and changes. Learning from past experience, and from the experience of others, becomes essential to avoid wasting resources, time and political capital in the arduous long-term process of building endogenous science and technology capabilities. This puts a high premium on having a highly qualified group of policy-makers in this field, and also of ensuring that those in charge of policy making in related areas are aware of the importance of building science, technology and innovation capabilities.

5.4   THE REPERTOIRE OF POLICIES AND POLICY INSTRUMENTS

There is a vast repertoire of possible government interventions to foster the generation, acquisition, dissemination and utilization of scientific and technological knowledge, most of which have been devised and tried out in developed countries. The past three decades have also seen a growing interest in many developing countries in the range of policy instruments that can be used to build endogenous science and technology capabilities, and in the overall strategies that articulate their deployment.[5] The emergence of the concept of national systems of innovation and its application to developing country situations, particularly during the 1990s, has helped to focus attention on the institutional arrangements and policy interventions to promote innovation.

The conceptual model advanced in this book (Chapter 1, Figure 1.1) can be used to identify the main categories of policy instruments to create an endogenous science and technology base, which are now available to policy- and decision-makers in developing countries (Table 5.1). The first category comprises *government interventions aimed at building science, technology and innovation capacities*; the second includes *measures that focus on the creation of linkages between domestic science and technology and those at the global level*, and particularly in developed countries; and the third category comprises actions to *establish a favorable context and an appropriate institutional framework for the creation of scientific research, technological development and innovation capacities*.

There are several other ways of identifying and classifying government interventions to promote the creation and consolidation of endogenous science and technology capabilities. For example, one of the more elaborate schemes to examine 'market stimulating technology policies' in the industrial sector is that of Sanjaya Lall and Morris Teubal,[6] who consider three broad types of policy instruments: functional, which are intended to improve the functioning of markets (with emphasis on factor markets) but without favoring any particular set of production activities; vertical, which are selective policies

Table 5.1   Categories of government interventions to establish an endogenous science and technology base

Category	Type of policy instruments	Specific measures
Building science, technology and innovation capacities in developing countries	Supply side: creating science and technology institutions and building research and technology development capacities	Creation and consolidation of all types of science and technology institutions, financing of science and technology activities, human resource development, foresight and planning, creation of networks of institutions
	Demand side: promoting the utilization of domestic scientific and technological knowledge in production and service activities	Strategic planning of production and service activities, financing of innovation at the firm level, use of the state's purchasing power, technical norms and standards, fiscal incentives to stimulate innovation, promoting export of technology intensive goods
	Linking the domestic supply with the demand for science and technology knowledge associated with innovation in the production system	Science and technology parks and incubators, technology extension services, engineering design and consulting services, selective recovering and upgrading of traditional techniques, policies to promote technology diffusion between firms, cluster policies to link technology leaders with other firms
	Strengthening science and technology policy-making	Creation of specialized policy agencies, coordination of national and local initiatives, establishing of policy research and foresight centers, provide information to policy-makers
Creating linkages between knowledge, technology and production in developing countries and their global counterparts	Establishing linkages with the world scientific research community	Joint research projects, access to international science and technology information, remote access to research facilities and equipment, gathering data about natural resources and biodiversity, monitoring climate change and natural disasters

Table 5.1   continued

Category	Type of policy instruments	Specific measures
	Obtaining and securing access to external sources of technology	Purchase of technology intensive goods and services, technology licensing agreements, utilize intellectual property regulations, technology scanning and search
	Establishing linkages with the global production system	Direct foreign investment, import and export of equipment and machinery, trade in goods and services, subcontracting in global value chains
Establishing a favorable context and institutional framework for creating an endogenous science and technology base	Providing the physical infrastructure for the performance of scientific research, technology development and innovation	Communications facilities, transport infrastructure (roads, railroads, ports, airports), reliable energy supply (electricity, oil, gas), clean water and sanitation, waste disposal, clean air, appropriate land use regulations
	Establishing institutional arrangements favorable to innovation	Elimination of bureaucratic impediments, transparency, fair and effective regulatory agencies, prevalence of the rule of law, democratic governance
	Creating a stable economic policy framework conducive to long-term thinking in firms and other organizations	Price, interest rate and exchange rate stability, sensible financial and credit policies, prudent fiscal policies, tax arrangements that encourage investment, openness to trade and investment
	Evolving a cultural and social environment that encourages creativity, risk-taking and innovative behavior	General and scientific education, fair and flexible labor policies, environmental protection, access to information and freedom of the press, poverty and inequality reduction, punish corruption, encourage trust and build social capital, promote values congruent with modern entrepreneurship

Source: Prepared by the author.

aimed at fostering learning and capacities in specific areas of production; and horizontal, which comprises policies that support technology development independently of the sector or the technology. In addition, they classify market stimulating technology policies into three groups – priorities, incentives and institutions – and also point out that there are three levels or phases of policies: national level, priority setting level and specific programs/policies. These categories are interrelated and emphasize the systemic nature of policy design and implementation aimed at building endogenous science and technology capabilities. Lall and Teubal offer examples of policies drawn primarily from South-East Asia, Europe and North America, most of which coincide with the list of government interventions examined below.

The scheme used here aims at focusing, first, on those government interventions aimed at the supply–linkages–demand nexus that are essential for the generation, diffusion and utilization of technologies; second at those measures which improve the interactions between domestic knowledge, technology and production and their counterparts in other parts of the world, particularly in the technologically advanced nations; and third, at the set of policy interventions to create an enabling cultural, social and political context, together with an institutional infrastructure, that will foster the generation of knowledge of all types and stimulate the process of innovation.

Building Science, Technology and Innovation Capacities

This category of policy instruments has four main components: supply-side measures that aim at building institutions and capacities to produce scientific and technological knowledge, and also to recover and upgrade traditional knowledge and techniques; demand-side interventions to promote the utilization of domestically generated knowledge in production and service activities; measures to strengthen the linkages between the supply and demand of domestically produced or adapted knowledge; and actions to strengthen science and technology policy making capabilities.

The *supply-side component* of a strategy to build endogenous science and technology comprises institution building (creation, reorganization and consolidation of science and technology research centers; strengthening of university, government and independent laboratories; establishment of science support institutions including libraries, information centers, laboratory maintenance and repair facilities, metrology institutions, and calibration and standardization services); financing of science and technology activities (direct public budget support, special funds for research, endowments for foundations, competitive grants, block grants, research and services contracts, foreign bilateral assistance grants, loans from international financial institutions, tax incentives for private firms, venture capital); human resources development (fellowship programs, internships in the country and abroad, small grants for individual research and dissertation projects, science education programs in schools, expansion of higher education programs and facilities for science and technology, creating engineering sciences careers, specialized graduate programs for technology management, sabbatical leave programs for researchers, short-term courses given by high-level foreign specialists); science and technology foresight and planning (analysis of trends and potential developments in science and technology, definition of strategies for research and innovation in selected areas, identification of activities that should be given priority in resource allocation, dissemination of information on trends, strategies and policies); and fostering networking among science and technology institutions (establish multidisciplinary scientific research and technological development programs, create linkages between public and private research centers, foster interactions between institutions through periodic events and seminars).

The *demand side component* of the strategy to build an endogenous science and technology base comprises the measures that foster productive sector demands for locally produced science and technology knowledge. It includes encouraging technology management and planning activities in firms (dissemination of information on measures to improve competitiveness and increase productivity, technical assistance on how to make use of existing domestic knowledge and select the most appropriate external sources of knowledge, technical assistance to improve technology choices in firms); financing of innovation in firms (venture capital, subsidized loans and matching grants to purchase technology-intensive goods and services, tax exemptions and accelerated depreciation of capital goods and high-technology equipment, financing of special training programs for workers and professionals, working capital for experimentation and trial production runs); financing for technology institutions to participate in innovation (lines of credit for domestic engineering and consulting firms, funds for technology development and fine-tuning of processes and products, matching grants for the provision of technical assistance to firms); use of the purchasing power of the state to encourage demand for domestic technology (preference for local suppliers of technology and engineering services in bidding contests, direct contracts with local firms and research centers, purchase guarantees for manufacturers of technology intensive goods); technical norms and standards services (metrology laboratories, quality control programs, public–private partnerships to promote and enforce compliance with standards); and promoting exports of technology intensive goods and services (provision of information on potential export markets, credit lines for exports of machinery and equipment, financing arrangements for suppliers of engineering and consulting services, publicity campaigns to create demand for exports of technology intensive goods, tax credits and rebates for exporters, technical assistance for exports to meet international quality control and environmental standards).

The component of the strategy that aims at *establishing linkages between the domestic supply and the demand for scientific and technological knowledge associated with innovation* comprises 'push' measures that reach out from research institutions towards the production sector, 'pull' measures for enterprises to draw on domestic sources of knowledge, and measures that encourage the flow of knowledge throughout the production sector. These include establishing technology parks and incubators (associated with public research institutions, technical universities, private research centers); providing technology extension services (subsidized and free technical assistance programs for small and medium enterprises, specialized technical information centers, programs to improve productivity); encouraging engineering design and consulting firms (matching funds and preferential credit for firms to work with domestic engineers and consultants, support for professional associations and engineering events, preference for local consultants in public procurement); identifying, selecting and upgrading traditional techniques (inventories of indigenous techniques and products, research on traditional practices and production methods, technology blending programs); and promoting technology diffusion between enterprises (subcontracting and close relations with suppliers, fostering the creation of clusters of enterprises around a technological leader).

The *science and technology policy component* includes the establishment of science and technology policy-making bodies (national councils for science and technology, ministries of science and technology, coordinating commissions, advisory boards, office of the chief government scientist, parliamentary committees, technology assessment agencies); coordination of national and subnational policies (joint boards, national–local advisory bodies, special joint funds and programs); establishing research and teaching programs in science and technology policy (technology foresight centers, technology management courses, policy research units, graduate programs, periodic conferences and events, funds for policy research); and providing information services to policy makers (policy briefs, evaluation units, national science and technology budgets, inventories of science and technology capabilities).

Creating Linkages between Knowledge, Technology and Production in Developing Countries and their Global Counterparts

This category of policy instruments has three components: establishing linkages between scientific research in the country and the international research community, securing access to the world sources of technology and establishing linkages between the domestic production system and its global counterparts.

The component of the strategy that aims at *linking the domestic and global scientific research communities* includes organizing and carrying out joint research projects (twinning programs between universities, collaboration between research centers, networks of developed and developing country institutions); ensuring access to international scientific and technological information (subscriptions to scientific research data bases, agreements between libraries in developed and developing countries, exchange of publications); remote access to research facilities and equipment (time sharing agreements for using sophisticated laboratory equipment, on-line connections with data-processing facilities, creating virtual research communities); data-gathering initiatives for the international research community (mapping natural resource availability, biodiversity prospecting, monitoring climate change and natural disasters, harmonizing data-gathering protocols); and organizing exchanges of views between researchers (visiting fellowships, regular international conferences and symposia, sabbatical programs).

The component of the strategy that focuses on *securing access to the international sources of technology* includes measures to promote the importation of technology-intensive goods and services (purchase of high-technology products, monitoring of and linking with new technology developments, reverse engineering, contracts with foreign engineering and consulting firms); technology licensing agreements (monitoring and evaluating international licensing trends, providing technical assistance to firms negotiating technology agreements, adopting national legislation to encourage licensing); and organizing technology scanning and search services (technology missions to foreign countries, technical assistance to help small and medium enterprises find technology sources, training programs for technology purchasers).

The component that deals with *establishing linkages with the global production systems* aims at improving the competitiveness of the developing country and its firms, and also at seeking a more active participation in world trade, finance and technology flows. It includes the promotion of direct foreign investment (information on investment opportunities, incentives to foreign investors); promotion of trade in technology intensive goods (removal of tariffs, tax rebates for the re-export of manufactured goods, credit lines and guarantees for technology imports and exports); promoting the participation of domestic firms in global value chains (identification of potential opportunities, technical and financial assistance for domestic firms, cluster policies and subcontracting, incentives to establish strategic alliances with foreign firms).

Establishing a Favorable Context for Scientific Research, Technological Development and Innovation

This category includes four main groups of policy instruments: providing the physical infrastructure required for science, technology and innovation; creating institutional arrangements favorable to innovation; maintaining a stable economic framework that promotes investment and long-term thinking in science, technology and production; and evolving a cultural and social environment that encourages creativity, risk-taking, and innovative behavior.

The component dealing with the *provision of physical infrastructure* includes measures to install telecommunication networks (widespread access to low-cost fixed and mobile telephone services, reliable digital data transmission networks, massive access to the Internet, incentives for the acquisition of information technology equipment); to construct and maintain transport facilities (highways and secondary roads, ports, airports, railroads); to ensure a reliable supply of energy (electricity generation plants and transmission networks, steady supply of hydrocarbon fuels, renewable energy generation sources in remote areas); to provide access to clean water and sanitation (water treatment plants, water distribution networks, regulations on the use of groundwater, water recycling facilities); to make available waste disposal facilities (waste treatment plants, landfills, special facilities and regulations for toxic waste); and to reduce air pollution (measures to reduce the discharge of pollutants into the air, programs to reduce greenhouse gas emissions).

The component that refers to the *institutional arrangements favorable to innovation* includes the elimination of bureaucratic impediments that affect firms and other institutions (administrative simplification, single-window procedures to approve programs and plans, reducing administrative requirements for operation); ensuring transparency in central and local government operations (full disclosure of information, access to the budgets of public agencies, well-defined bidding procedures for public sector procurement); fair and effective regulatory agencies (autonomy of regulatory agencies, well-defined regulation procedures, contracts for the provision of public services, special training programs for regulators); full prevalence of the rule of law (independence of the Judiciary, Congress and the Executive, stability of legal frameworks, well-functioning legal system); and democratic governance (fair and free elections, democratic habits of thought and practice, similar treatment for all economic agents and individuals, measures to build investor confidence).

The component that deals with establishing a *stable economic policy framework that encourages long-term thinking and innovation* includes appropriate macroeconomic policies (maintain price stability and low inflation rates, ensure currency convertibility and a stable exchange rate, keep adequate levels of foreign exchange reserves, Central Bank autonomy); financial and credit policies (well-functioning financial system, interest rates not too far from the international cost of money, fair collateral requirements for loans, expedient bankruptcy procedures); fiscal policies that encourage investment (tax incentives for reinvesting profits, tax credits for equipment upgrading, accelerated depreciation, tariff reductions for the import of technology-intensive machinery); openness to trade and investment (low tariffs, simple and stable rules for foreign investors, harmonization of developing country policies to avoid a 'race to the bottom' when attracting foreign investment, regional agreements to establish free trade zones and common markets).

Finally, the component of a strategy for building endogenous science and technology capabilities that deal with *evolving a cultural and social environment that encourages creativity, risk taking, responsibility and innovation* comprises a broad range of policies and policy interventions. These include general and scientific education (reform of primary and secondary education, priority for technical education, scientific literacy programs, distance and remedial education programs for workers, reorientation of the higher education system towards scientific and technical careers, programs to create a public informed about science and technology matters); fair and flexible labor policies (balancing labor mobility with protection of workers, technical training programs for workers in transition from one job to another, measures to encourage the mobility of highly qualified workers and technicians); environmental protection measures (resource and energy conservation policies, incentives to adopt environment friendly technologies, special funds and credit lines to support pollution abating initiatives); access to information and freedom of the press (provision of adequate information to citizens, promotion of probing and responsible behavior of the press, encourage tolerance and the free exchange of ideas); measures to reduce inequalities (access to basic social services, poverty reduction programs, employment generation initiatives, measures to ensure gender equity); exposing and punishing corruption (penalties for taking and giving bribes, banishment of corrupt firms from deals with public entities, barring corrupt politicians from taking part in elections, incentives for 'whistle blowers' and others who denounce corrupt acts); and measures to encourage trust, build social capital and promote democratic values that are congruent with modern science and technology (educational campaigns, prizes for innovators, public recognition of contributions by citizens and organizations).

This broad repertoire of policies and policy instruments comprises a large number of possible direct and indirect government interventions to build endogenous science and technology capabilities. Not all of them are equally important to all developing countries, and the choice of interventions has to be adapted to their historical evolution, present situation and development strategy.

Policies and policy instruments have different information, organizational and administrative capacity requirements. Some of them work in clusters and reinforce each other while others work individually and may lead to inconsistencies and contradictions. There are interventions that aim at influencing the behavior of agents in the science, technology and innovation system in a general way, and others that focus on a specific aspect of their behavior. Some policy instruments have an immediate impact, while others take a longer time to filter through the administrative apparatus of the government and their influence is felt with considerable delay. In addition, policies and policy instruments are just some of the many factors that influence the behavior of researchers, professionals, managers, entrepreneurs and government officials who are involved in the science, technology and innovation system. Their background, preferences and objectives, together with market structures, institutional incentives, technological trajectories, capabilities of firms, and the specific characteristics of the technology and of production activities, are among the many other factors that influence scientific, technological and innovative behavior. These are all rather independent of the purposeful interventions of government entities.

Therefore, the choice of policy and policy instruments is a complex task that has to keep in mind their appropriateness, impact, effectiveness, congruence and efficiency, as well as their flexibility and capacity to adapt to changing circumstances. The concept of 'capacity-building' acquires a different meaning in each of the three categories of developing countries identified by using the Science and Technology Capacity Index (Chapter 4, Section 4.2), and even within a particular category it will be necessary to tailor the strategies, policies and instruments to the conditions prevailing in a specific country.

The classification of developing countries into three categories using the Science and Technology Capacity Index can be used to illustrate the relevance of the various policy instruments to countries with different levels of science and technology capabilities. Table 5.2 presents a list of policy instruments with observations about their relative importance to Type II, Type III and Type IV developing countries. The lower the level of science and technology capabilities, the greater the importance of policy instruments orientated towards creating the basic institutional infrastructure for scientific research, technological development and innovation. Conversely, for the relatively more advanced developing countries, those policies that improve competitiveness and build linkages with global science, technology and innovation become more important.

Table 5.2   Policies and policy instruments by categories of developing countries: illustrative relevance according to their Science and Technology (S&T) Capacity Index

Policies	Policy instruments	TYPE II	TYPE III	TYPE IV
Building science, technology and innovation capacities in developing countries:				
Supply-side measures: building science and technology infrastructure	Institution building	++	++	+++
	Financing of science and technology activities	+++	++	++
	Human resources development	++	+++	+++
	Defining science and technology priorities and plans	+	+++	++
	Creating networks of science and technology institutions	++	+++	++
Demand-side measures: promoting the application of knowledge	Strategic planning of production activities	++	+++	+
	Financing of innovation and the purchase of technology intensive good and services	+++	++	+
	Use of the purchasing power of the State	+	+++	++
	Fiscal measures to stimulate innovation at the firm level	+++	++	+
	Measures to promote the export of technology intensive goods and services	+++	++	+
Measures to strengthen the linkage between supply and demand of science and technology knowledge	Policies to promote diffusion of technologies	++	+++	+++
	Cluster-related policies to link technology and production	+	+++	++
	Engineering design and consulting services	+++	++	+
	Norms, standards, and quality control	+++	+++	++
	Selective recovery upgrading of traditional technologies	+	+++	+
	Science and technology parks and technology incubators	+++	++	+
	Technology extension services	+	+++	++
Measures to strengthen the science and technology policy making capacities	Creation of specialized agency in charge of science and technology	+++	++	+
	Coordination of local and regional initiatives to promote science and technology	+++	++	+
	Promoting international agreements and cooperation	+++	+++	+++
	Establishing science and technology forecasting centers	++	++	+
	Providing information to science and technology policy and decision makers	++	++	+++
Creating linkages between knowledge, technology and production in developing countries and their counterparts at the global level:				
Linkages between the global and the domestic science systems	Joint research activities	++	+++	++
	Access to international science and technology information	++	+++	++
	Remote access to research facilities and equipment	+	++	+
	Mapping natural resources, climate change, epidemics, disaster, biodiversity, etc.	+	++	++

Category	Item			
Linkages with the external sources of technology	Purchasing of technology and technological services	+++	++	+
	Technical and engineering design assistance	+++	++	+
	International intellectual property agreements	+++	+++	++
	Technology scanning and search	+++	+++	++
Linkages with the global production system	Import and export of equipment, machinery and goods	++	+++	++
	Promotion of foreign direct investment	+++	+++	++
	Improving competitiveness and productivity	++	+++	+
Establishing a favorable context and institutional framework:				
Providing physical infra-structure for science and technology and innovation	Communication	+	++	+++
	Develop transport infrastructure	+	++	+++
	Reliable provision of energy	+	++	+++
	Provision of clean water, sanitation and waste disposal facilities	+	++	+++
Creating institutional arrangements favorable to innovation	Democratic governance	++	+++	++
	Legal framework	+++	++	+
	Competition policies	+++	++	+
	Reduce bureaucratic impediments	+++	++	++
	Protect intellectual property rights	+++	++	++
Creating a conducive and stable economic policy framework	Stable macroeconomic environment	+++	+++	+++
	Financial and credit policies	++	+++	++
	Fiscal policies	+++	++	+
	Trade openness	+++	++	+
Evolving a cultural and social environment that encourages creativity, risk-taking, responsibility and innovation	Labor policies	+++	++	++
	General education	++	++	+++
	Environmental protection	+++	++	++
	Access to information	++	++	++
	Poverty reduction initiatives and reducing inequality	+	++	+++
	Ensuring freedom of initiative and encouraging creativity	+++	+++	+++
	Measures to encourage trust and build social capital	++	++	+++

Notes:
(+) Not relevant. (+ +) Moderately relevant. (+ + +) Highly relevant.

Source: Prepared by the author.

5.5   A ROLE FOR INTERNATIONAL COOPERATION

The international community plays a critical role in the creation of endogenous science and technology capabilities in developing countries. The preceding chapters have indicated that it is not possible to develop domestic scientific research, technological development and innovation capacities in isolation, without continuous and intensive interactions with the world's science, technology and innovation systems.

However, not all types of external linkages contribute to the creation of an endogenous science and technology base, and some of them can undermine efforts to do so. For example, an active involvement with the international scientific community may lead developing country scientists to lose sight of the problems faced in their own regions, primarily because prestige and financial incentives are biased towards research on topics of interest to the developed countries, because the emigration of qualified scientists reduces the possibility of accumulating a critical mass of highly qualified personnel, and because the choice of research themes with little impact on development creates an 'internal brain drain'. Restrictions on the use of imported technologies imposed by their owners curtail options for firms and can also block interactions between those technologies and domestic scientific and technological research. Close relations between international and domestic enterprises can exclude or limit the participation of developing country engineering, consulting and technology services firms in the process of innovation.

These examples indicate that some types of external linkages keep domestic knowledge, technology and production apart from each other, and may hamper the creation of an endogenous science and technology base. Moreover, discoveries and knowledge generated in developing countries could be appropriated by developed country researchers and firms, and even find their way back to their place of origin as costly technology packages. Controversies regarding intellectual property rights and the patenting of indigenous medicinal plants by transnational pharmaceutical corporations suggest that this is not a far-fetched idea.

Therefore, the task is to forge appropriate and mutually beneficial linkages between knowledge, technology and production in the developing countries and their counterparts at the global level. There are several ways in which such links could be established. For example, research networks can help institutions in both groups of countries to join forces in the generation of knowledge. Fields like tropical biology, health sciences, ecology and the environment and information sciences, among many others, lend themselves to this approach, and even some of the basic sciences (theoretical physics, mathematics, astronomy) would also qualify. Networks of technological alliances between public institutions and private firms from both developed and developing countries can also be mutually beneficial, as in the case of consulting activities, the provision of technical services and the adaptation of technologies to local conditions, especially in fields like natural resources and agriculture, where access to domestic sources of knowledge is essential and the participation of local professionals can reduce costs. Similar remarks apply to joint ventures between foreign and domestic firms, as in the case of clusters of enterprises of various sizes where large foreign investors establish links with small and medium-size local production and service units. Domestic firms benefit from the technical assistance and the demand for their products and services, while the large foreign firms secure local supply sources at lower cost and generate goodwill in the process.

In addition to solidarity, respect and a positive disposition from members of the scientific and technological communities, forging mutually beneficial linkages with developing country institutions requires a favorable attitude on the part of government authorities and private sector managers in developed countries. A broader conception of 'enlightened self-interest', which incorporates support for the creation of endogenous science and technology capabilities, should inform foreign investment and development assistance programs.

However, in spite of the key role that the international community can play in the development of endogenous scientific and technological capabilities, public and private agencies in developed countries, as well as international institutions, have shown relatively little interest in raising international cooperation in science and technology to a level commensurate with their importance in development. The exceptions are a few private foundations (Rockefeller, MacArthur, Packard, Ford, Carnegie Corporation, Wellcome Trust, Gates Foundation and, more recently, Moore and Lemelson), some scientific associations in developed countries and at the international level (United States National Academy of Sciences, Third World Academy of Sciences), and special agencies, such as the Canadian International Development Research Centre (IDRC) and the Netherlands' Development Research Assistance Council (RAWOO), which were created specifically for this purpose.

A few private firms have established in-house foundations that support activities in regions and fields related to their commercial interests, such as the foundation created by Shell Corporation to support research on sustainable energy and environmental conservation. Several international organizations, including the United Nations Development Programme (UNDP), the World Health Organization (WHO), the United Nations Educational, Scientific and Cultural Organization (UNESCO), the United Nations Conference on Trade and Development (UNCTAD) and the United Nations Industrial Development Organization (UNIDO), have been active in the field of international cooperation in science and technology, but the scale of their efforts is limited by woefully inadequate budgets and large administrative overheads.

Multilateral development banks have been active in providing loans for establishing and upgrading research facilities in developing countries, mostly associated with programs to support tertiary education. The Inter-American Development Bank has been providing loans for this purpose since its creation in 1959, and the World Bank has also been active in this field, although to a proportionally lower extent given its size and resources. Finally, some universities and non-governmental associations in developed countries have also organized international cooperation programs of their own, the first centered around fellowships and joint research projects, and the second focusing on training and the transfer of specific technologies (for example, the Intermediate Technology Development Group in the United Kingdom).

A recent inventory of international science and technology cooperation programs[7] identified more than 250 initiatives under way in the early 2000s, but the vast majority of these are rather small and have very limited funds, or they have other purposes and science and technology play a minor role in their activities. They range over a wide variety of fields and regions, focus on different aspects of the process of building endogenous science and technology capabilities, and operate without coordination. The general picture that emerges is one of limited, widely dispersed and possibly unsustainable science and technology cooperation programs that, even when taken as a whole, fall short of what would be required to assist developing countries in the Sisyphean task of building their endogenous science and technology capabilities.

In spite of the relatively limited magnitude and impact of international science and technology cooperation programs, many valuable lessons of experience can be drawn from the activities of private foundations and development assistance agencies (Box 5.1). These lessons suggest ways of designing new international cooperation programs, mechanisms and institutions that could measure up to the challenge of mobilizing knowledge and innovation to improve the human condition.

The limited impact of the large number of scattered and undersized international science and technology cooperation initiatives contrasts with the periodic calls made in a variety of regional and global forums, and particularly in the United Nations, to expand development assistance in this field. The first United Nations Conference on Science and Technology for the Benefit of the Less-developed Nations was held in Geneva in 1963, and its final declaration argued that science and technology provided short cuts to development and can help to reduce the gap between rich and poor countries. A leading participant in that event (Nobel Prize winner Lord P.M.S. Blackett), used the analogy of a 'supermarket' of scientific and technological achievements

BOX 5.1   INTERNATIONAL SUPPORT FOR SCIENCE AND TECHNOLOGY IN DEVELOPING COUNTRIES: A SUMMARY OF BEST PRACTICES

A feasibility study for the establishment of a 'European Science and Technology for Development Foundation' has identified a list of best practices for foundations, development assistance agencies and international organizations to follow:

- Support for science and technology in developing countries requires *a clearly enunciated goal* with attendant thoughts on how to measure progress toward that goal. Most foundations and development agencies describe their focus in sweeping and vague terms such as 'to empower the citizens of the world', 'to eliminate global poverty, inequality and injustice, to promote public involvement in civic affairs', which make it impossible to measure either success or failure.
- Significant change is rarely easy or quick and *long-term commitment* is required. Institutions, cultural patterns, laws, and values change slowly. The experience of the past 30 years demonstrates amply that very few programs are successful if they do not have staying power. The most successful of the foundation programs have taken decades to realize their potential.
- *Scale and critical mass* must be taken into account. Successful support programs have taken seriously the requirement to match resources with problems. Real progress on any significant issue requires large amounts of money; it is impossible to build or test any significant theory or to bring about major capabilities without a funding scale that relates to the problem.
- *Patience and tolerance of errors* are essential. Capacity-building does not occur without mistakes and disappointments. To be effective it is necessary to learn how to embrace error. Foundations have a particular comparative advantage in this connection. Compared with governmental and intergovernmental organizations, the flexibility of foundations affords them a major advantage in capacity-building.

- *Follow-through and systemic approaches* are required. Long-term support is one thing, but follow-through is quite another. A major lesson from previous experience has been that support for science without support for technology and innovation has limited significantly the benefits that have resulted. Foundations, bilateral agencies and international organizations can forever seed new programs and then jump on to newer subjects. Seeding new programs is indeed exciting, but unless someone is around to water the seedlings, weed them, harvest the grain and bake the bread, seeding itself is useless.
- *Risk-taking* is increasing among the newer and better foundations. Funders interested in supporting new approaches and ventures have identified a need for this sector to take greater risk in its work. This involves financing start-up ventures, new entrepreneurs and projects that take bold approaches to achieving social and environmental objectives.
- *Leadership development* is key, as good people are at the heart of most successful programs and projects. There is a growing trend for new funders to recognize and finance outstanding talent.

Source: Extracted and adapted from Bezanson and Oldham (2000).

generated by the developed nations, where developing countries could easily find solutions 'off the shelf'. This analogy would be shown to be inappropriate in subsequent decades, among other reasons because intellectual property rights biased in favor of technology owners makes it costly and difficult to gain access to the 'shelves' of the science and technology 'supermarket'.

The imbalances in science and technology capabilities between developed and developing countries were already visible at that time, and prompted calls to use the scientific and technological capacities of the former to address the problems of the latter. The 1970 'World Plan of Action on Science and Technology for Development', prepared by the United Nations Advisory Committee on Science and Technology (ACAST) created at the Geneva Conference, proposed that 5 per cent of research and development expenditures in rich countries should be focused on the problems of poor nations. However, with the minor exception of a few fields such as medical research and health care, the mobilization of developed country scientists to focus on the problems of the developing world has not been very successful.

This proposal highlighted one of the key problems in international science and technology cooperation. Scientific research and technological development in the developed nations can be used to solve specific developing country problems in the short term, but this would not necessarily help to build domestic capabilities in the medium and long term. It is not possible to assume that the twin objectives of capacity-building and problem-solving can be achieved simultaneously and without conflict. There are urgent demands that require science and technology solutions, and which cannot wait for the relatively lengthy process of building domestic capabilities to satisfy those urgencies later – for example, developing vaccines to prevent malaria and other tropical diseases. Other situations require capacity building efforts first, so as to enable the local scientific and technological community to address problems in a continuous and sustainable manner – for example, developing low cost technologies to satisfy basic needs such as sanitation, housing, primary health care, nutrition and elementary education, all of which must be tailored to local conditions. Box 5.2 highlights some of the tensions and dilemmas between problem-solving and capacity-building.

A second United Nations Conference on Science and Technology for Development (UNCSTD) took place in 1979 in Vienna. The years since the 1963 event saw a change in the optimistic view that science and technology are a positive force for development, and rather than focusing primarily on using 'off the shelf' technologies from developed countries the Vienna Program of Action emphasized the importance of building endogenous science and technology capabilities. This program of action created a United Nations Financing System for Science and Technology for Development (UNFSSTD) made up of voluntary contributions, which was supposed and reach an annual level of US$250 million. The financing system did not materialize in the confrontational international climate of the early 1980s, and was replaced by an Interim Fund for Science and Technology for Development within the United Nations Development Programme. This Interim Fund never succeeded in generating more than a fraction of the resources envisioned in Vienna and languished for a long time before being dismantled in the early 1990s.

Another appeal to revitalize international cooperation in science and technology for development was made in the late 1980s, on the occasion of the tenth anniversary of the Vienna Conference. The members of the United Nations Advisory Committee on Science and Technology for Development issued a declaration pointing out that humanity approached the new century and new millennium confronting a fundamental paradox: 'we have never had so much power to influence the course of civilization, to shape the way our species will evolve, and to create an ever-expanding range of opportunities for human betterment – but we remain unwilling or unable to use this new-found power to achieve our full potential as human beings' (see Appendix 2).

BOX 5.2   INTERACTIONS BETWEEN CAPACITY-
BUILDING AND PROBLEM-SOLVING IN
INTERNATIONAL SCIENCE AND
TECHNOLOGY COOPERATION
PROGRAMS

Motivations for international cooperation programs to focus on science and technology issues usually have two sets of objectives: (i) to solve a specific problem (develop vaccines, improve crop yields, provide educational materials); and (ii) to build capacity for developing countries to be able to solve problems on their own (create research institutions, provide fellowships, support local technology development efforts, give access to information). These two objectives are associated to different degrees in specific programs and interventions.

At one extreme, it is possible to use the scientific research and technology development capabilities of developed countries, for example in leading North American and European laboratories or universities, to generate knowledge, technologies and products that address the problem under consideration. This may take a relatively short time and have a higher probability of success than alternative approaches, but would not assist the developing country in building the capacity to address similar problems in the future. The effectiveness of this approach will depend on the problem area, the state of scientific and technological knowledge, and the familiarity of researchers in developed countries with the problem being addressed.

At the other extreme, it is possible to support the creation of domestic science, technology and innovation capabilities in a developing country, which may involve institutional support programs, long-term scientific and technical assistance, information sharing, and graduate fellowships to train science and technology researchers, as well as policy-makers and technology managers. This approach takes a relatively long time and has lower probability of success in addressing specific immediate problems than the alternative, but would put in place the capabilities for developing countries to confront their own problems in the future. The effectiveness of this approach will depend on the commitment of the political leaders, on the existence of a supporting policy environment, and on the availability of resources to support science, technology and innovation initiatives.

Between these two extremes there is a range of intermediate approaches that involve, to varying degrees, combinations of problem-solving and capacity-building programs. The interactions between the two objectives and the programs that support them are rather complex and can be depicted in the following graph. Lines (a), (b) and (c) depict programs that build capacity as they solve problems, although to different degrees. Line (d) suggests that it is necessary to have a minimum level of local capacity before problem-solving can be attempted, while line (e) suggests that it is necessary first to solve the problem before capacity can be built. These are cases of positive association between problem-solving and capacity-building, and a whole set of curves could be drawn to indicate, for example, diminishing marginal returns to capacity building in relation to problem-solving, or the opposite. There may be cases in which these two objectives involve trade-offs and choices must be made between capacity-building and problem-solving. Line (f) depicts such an unfortunate situation.

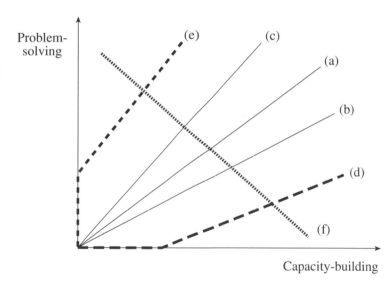

Source: Prepared by the author.

The declaration ended with a call to develop during the 1990s 'a multiplicity of innovative approaches to bilateral, regional and global cooperation in science and technology for development', which went unheeded.

The beginning of the 21st century appears to be an appropriate time for another attempt at launching a major international effort to mobilize science and technology for development. This is partly because of the growing awareness of the emergence of the knowledge society, and because imbalances in science and technology capabilities have reached alarming levels – and still keep on growing. A four-pronged effort will be required to place knowledge and innovation at center stage in development efforts.

First, it will be necessary to launch a major global communications and information campaign to highlight the importance of science and technology for development. The aim should be to persuade political, business and civil society leaders, as well as citizens in general, that building endogenous science and technology capabilities in developing countries is a high-priority task for the international community. Without broad citizen support and pressure from a variety of stakeholders interested in mobilizing knowledge for development, it will be most difficult for leaders to take major initiatives in this field. The success of the environmental movement during the past three decades provides an illustration of what could and should be done with science and technology.

Second, considering the large number and dispersion of current international science and technology cooperation programs, better coordination and the harmonization of practices have become an imperative. The more than 250 programs identified in the inventory prepared by the Center for Global Studies at the University of Victoria suggest there is ample scope for improving the effectiveness of cooperation initiatives in this field, and possibly for the consolidation of several of these programs.

Third, it is essential to organize joint efforts between developing countries that often face the same problems, have similar resource endowments, experience comparable resource limitations and find it very difficult to acquire, on their own, the critical mass of capabilities needed to mobilize knowledge and innovation for improving living standards. In spite of the potential benefits of what is usually referred as 'technical cooperation between developing countries' (TCDC), there have been only sporadic initiatives to establish and sustain such programs. This is largely because of the lack of interest of public sector policy-makers, of the preference for researchers to work with their counterparts in developed nations, of the bias of the engineering community towards state-of-the-art technologies and of the predilection of production sector managers to establish ties with firms from developed countries. Direct foreign investment, technical assistance programs and collaborative research projects that originate in countries with an endogenous science and technology base (Type I countries according to the scheme of Chapter 4, Section 4.2) reinforce these North–South ties, at the expense of collaboration between developing countries. Yet there have been some efforts to organize 'triangular cooperation' arrangements, in which developed countries support relatively more advanced developing countries (Type II or III) and assist other developing countries with lower science and technology capabilities (those in Type III and IV).

Fourth, there is an urgent need to expand the level of resources allocated to help developing countries to build endogenous science and technology capabilities and to solve their specific problems. The magnitude of the knowledge divide (Table 4.1) indicates that this is an urgent task, and that the initiatives launched during the last three decades fall woefully short of meeting the Sisyphean challenge of mobilizing knowledge and innovation to improve the human condition. This will require innovative financial mechanisms and new institutional structures to raise, administer and channel a significant amount of resources.

The characteristics of such arrangements can be exemplified through a proposal for the creation of a metaphoric 'global knowledge and development facility', which could become the first of a new generation of international financial institutions to promote international cooperation and development. The previous generation of such institutions – comprising the United Nations and its agencies, the multilateral development banks, the International Monetary Fund and the European Community, among others – emerged in the years following World War II. They should now be complemented by institutions attuned to the demands of the 21st century, and particularly with the need to bridge the knowledge divide between rich and poor nations. Based on what we have learned about financing international science and technology cooperation initiatives, Box 5.3 suggests some criteria for designing such a global knowledge and development facility.

The financial aspects of the facility should take into consideration that there is a new landscape for international development financing. Government sources of development assistance have stagnated during the last decade and have began to edge up only in 2002–03 for some countries such as the United Kingdom, France and, to a much lesser extent, the United States. It is unlikely that official sources will play in the near future the leading role in transfers to developing countries – as they did in the mid-1980s – except for the least developed countries. Moreover, the growing list of demands for official development assistance – humanitarian relief, debt reduction, support of economies in transition, halving world poverty by 2015 – may make it an uphill task to persuade bilateral agencies to support something like the metaphorical global knowledge and development facility outlined here.

The highly successful 50-year-old model of the multilateral development banks, which have mobilized a large amount of resources from private capital markets for development purposes, provides an indication of what could be done to establish new financial mechanisms to support science and technology

BOX 5.3   DESIGN CRITERIA FOR A 'GLOBAL
KNOWLEDGE AND DEVELOPMENT
FACILITY'

The creation of a global knowledge and development facility, which should be viewed as a set of interrelated financial and institutional mechanisms, should be guided by several design criteria that would ensure its relevance and impact. Among these criteria it is possible to identify:

Quantitative increase. The proposed facility should lead to a major increase in the amount of resources allocated to bridge the knowledge divide and to create endogenous science and technology capabilities in developing countries.

Diversity and differentiation. The proposed facility should be able to tailor its interventions to the characteristics of the developing countries, the economic and social sectors, and the type of science and technology activities involved.

Coordination and spread of best practice. The proposed facility should coordinate the large number of disparate initiatives currently under way. This implies promoting exchanges of views and experiences, organizing networks of researchers and practitioners, and disseminating best practices regarding science, technology and innovation policies, policy instruments, programs and organizations. To this end, the facility should sponsor regular seminars and training courses, briefings for policy-makers, and publications in printed and electronic media.

Flexibility and continuity. The proposed facility should balance the need for continuous evaluation and renewal on the one hand, with the need to maintain support for long periods on the other. One option is to organize the facility's activities on the basis of temporary programs of variable duration, subject to sunset clauses. The idea is to avoid the pitfall of creating permanent organizations that eventually outlive their usefulness, and that as time passes begin to answer to the concerns of their staff rather than those of their clients and beneficiaries.

Effective governance. The multiplicity of stakeholders involved in mobilizing knowledge for development requires innovative approaches to governance in the proposed facility. Procedures to ensure, transparency, accountability, participation and representation need to be carefully examined, so as to ensure the legitimacy of the facility and to ensure the necessary level of support from all stakeholders.

Existing and new elements. There are many initiatives under way which could eventually become closely associated with the proposed facility. It is important to allow room for accommodating the specific features of current initiatives, so as to incorporate them into the proposed facility. The facility should also specify clearly the characteristics of the new programs to be launched under its auspices.

Learning from similar initiatives. There are some precedents that provide useful points of reference for the proposed facility. The Global Environment Facility (GEF), launched by the World Bank, the United Nations Development Programme (UNDP) and the United Nations Environment Program (UNEP) more than a decade ago, and the Global Alliance for Vaccines and Immunization (GAVI) which puts together private foundations, government agencies and international institutions, offer valuable lessons for the design of the proposed facility.

Source: Prepared by the author.

in developing countries. The broad range of highly sophisticated financial instruments now available to individual and institutional investors – swaps, guarantees, derivatives, mutual funds and synthetic indexes, among many others – suggests that it should be possible to devise a set of instruments with the appropriate levels of risk and return for the proposed facility to tap into the vast amounts of private capital searching for investment opportunities. The idea would be to leverage grants from bilateral assistance agencies, foundations, developing country governments, private corporations, wealthy individuals and international institutions by using a portion of these resources to provide an appropriate and attractive level of comfort to private investors. This would allow a relatively modest initial amount of resources to increase significantly by accessing international capital markets.

The proposed facility should be able to take in contributions from different types of partners, some of which are likely to be in kind rather than in cash. Contributions should also be commensurate with the relative financial strengths of the partners. In addition, those responsible for the management of the proposed facility should be free from interference by political or commercial interests and be given autonomy to operate without excessive and cumbersome controls, but with clearly defined lines of accountability to all stakeholders participating in the scheme.

Moreover, there is also the possibility to link the proposed global knowledge and development facility to the growing international interest in the provision of global public goods. Knowledge is clearly a public good, at least in principle. As pointed out in Section 5.3 of this chapter, it is non-rivalrous (the use by one person or firm does not diminish the amount available to another) and it is also non-excludable (once it has been generated it is available to all).

Yet the institutional arrangements associated with intellectual property rights have been designed specifically to allow the private appropriation of knowledge, intrinsically a public good, and to create artificial scarcities of knowledge that generate temporary monopoly rents for its owners. The reasonable argument is that without such incentives private agents would not engage in the production of knowledge, which would then be undersupplied. This has been the main justification for establishing the international system of intellectual property rights and patents that has evolved over centuries, but which now requires urgent revision in order to create the conditions for bridging the knowledge divide between rich and poor nations.[8]

Financial arrangements for the provision of global public goods encompass a variety of mechanisms, which range from the creation of markets to direct government financing (Figure 5.1). Intellectual property rights create markets in which the users of knowledge pay its owners for licenses, patents and technical assistance. When markets are difficult to create, there are other mechanisms to finance the production of scientific and technological knowledge for development purposes (government budgets, grants from bilateral assistance agencies and private foundations, donations from individuals and private corporations, and loans from multilateral development banks, among others).

There is also a need for adopting new approaches to the identification, design and management of initiatives to support the mobilization of knowledge and innovation to improve the human condition. There should be an emphasis on problem oriented programs that involve many scientific disciplines and engineering fields; each program should be backed up by a coalition of relevant and concerned stakeholders, who should contribute according to their abilities and resources; programs should be temporary in nature, with specific organizational arrangements and sunset clauses; programs should be monitored and evaluated by independent external bodies; and there should be a small central unit in charge of identifying, designing and launching the programs (several of which would run simultaneously), but which would not be involved in their management.

During the last decade there has been a proliferation of partnership arrangements between bilateral agencies, foundations, international institutions, private corporations, civil society organizations and academic centers to

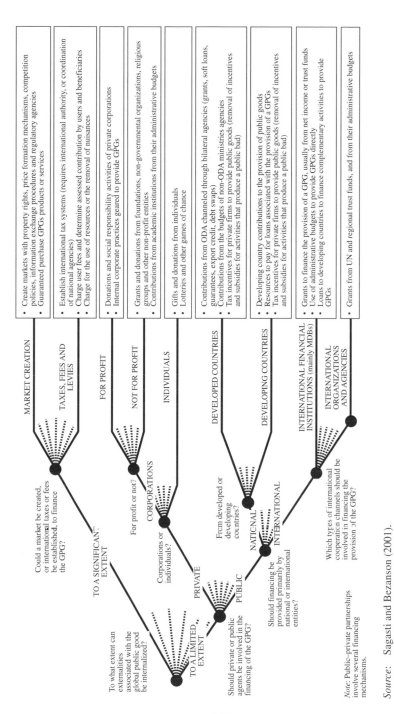

- Create markets with property rights, price formation mechanisms, competition policies, information exchange procedures and regulatory agencies
- Guaranteed purchase GPGs products or services

- Establish international tax systems (requires international authority, or coordination of national agencies)
- Charge user fees and determine assessed contribution by users and beneficiaries
- Charge for the use of resources or the removal of nuisances

- Donations and social responsibility activities of private corporations
- Internal corporate practices geared to provide GPGs

- Grants and donations from foundations, non-governmental organizations, religious groups and other non-profit entities
- Contributions from academic institutions from their administrative budgets

- Gifts and donations from individuals
- Lotteries and other games of chance

- Contributions from ODA channeled through bilateral agencies (grants, soft loans, guarantees, export credit, debt swaps)
- Contributions from the budgets of non-ODA ministries agencies
- Tax incentives for private firms to provide public goods (removal of incentives and subsidies for activities that produce a public bad)

- Developing country contributions to the provision of public goods
- Resources to pay for loans associated with the provision of a GPGs
- Tax incentives for private firms to provide public goods (removal of incentives and subsidies for activities that produce a public bad)

- Grants to finance the provision of a GPG, usually from net income or trust funds
- Use of administrative budgets to provide GPGs directly
- Loans to developing countries to finance complementary activities to provide GPGs

- Grants from UN and regional trust funds, and from their administrative budgets

MARKET CREATION

TAXES, FEES AND LEVIES

FOR PROFIT

NOT FOR PROFIT

INDIVIDUALS

DEVELOPED COUNTRIES

DEVELOPING COUNTRIES

INTERNATIONAL FINANCIAL INSTITUTIONS (mainly MDBs)

INTERNATIONAL ORGANIZATIONS AND AGENCIES

Could a market be created, or international taxes or fees be established, to finance the GPG?

TO A SIGNIFICANT EXTENT

For profit or not?

CORPORATIONS

Corporations or individuals?

From developed or developing countries?

NATIONAL

INTERNATIONAL

Should financing be provided primarily by national or international entities?

PRIVATE

PUBLIC

TO A LIMITED EXTENT

To what extent can externalities associated with the global public good be internalized?

Should private or public agents be involved in the financing of the GPG?

Which types of international cooperation channels should be involved in financing the provision of the GPG?

Note: Public–private partnerships involve several financing mechanisms.

Source: Sagasti and Bezanson (2001).

Figure 5.1 A framework for exploring financing options for the provision of global public goods (GPGs)

113

address specific development issues, such as the production of HIV/AIDS vaccines, biodiversity conservation and the elimination of some endemic tropical diseases, among many others. In addition, there have been some initiatives to change the way in which bilateral development assistance is provided to developing countries (sector programs, block grants, direct budget support, rewards for past performance). This suggests there may be a willingness to explore new arrangements to assist developing countries.

International cooperation can become a powerful force for the creation of endogenous science and technology capabilities in developing countries. Yet, it is still far from fulfilling its potential. New and bold initiatives are required to avoid the knowledge divide becoming an impassable abyss. A design along the lines of the global knowledge and development facility outlined here could help to turn that potential into an effective force for development, and in particular for supporting the Sisyphean challenge of creating endogenous science and technology capabilities in developing countries.

NOTES

1. See Bernal ([1937] 1967).
2. The model proposed in Chapter 2 of this book, the concepts of endogenous and exogenous science and technology base, the notions of explicit and implicit science and technology policies, and the ideas regarding the selective recovery of the traditional technological base were first introduced during this phase. See Herrera (1976) and Sagasti (1976b; 1977a; 1977b; 1978b; 1979a; 1981).
3. Knowledge satisfies the economic conditions for defining a public good: it is non-excludable in the sense that it is difficult and costly to exclude those who do not pay for it from consuming it, and non-rivalrous in the sense that any one person's consumption of the good has no effect on the amount of it available to others. See Sagasti and Bezanson (2001). See also Chapter 3, section 3.5, and note 8 below.
4. The 'double window of opportunity' created by the transition from one techno-economic paradigm to another (Chapter 3, Section 3.4 and Figure 3.1) provides an illustration of the need for both persistence and flexibility.
5. The first large-scale comparative exercise to examine the range of possible developing country government interventions in developing countries was the Science and Technology Policy Instruments (STPI) project, which was carried out in the early 1970s. It introduced the idea of explicit or direct and implicit or indirect science and technology policies, of the efficiency and effectiveness of policy instruments, contextual factors and compared the situation of ten developing countries (Sagasti, 1978b). Another project of the same type was conducted for the Caribbean countries a few years later (Girvan, 1984). A similar, but much broader exercise on strategies for science and technology was conducted in the late 1970s (Halty, 1986).
6. Lall and Teubal (1998).
7. See http://www.globalcentres.org/html/project1.html.
8. The Commission on Intellectual Property Rights (IPRs), established by the United Kingdom Department for International Development, has stressed the importance of redesigning IPRs to benefit developing countries. Its report states clearly the positive and negative aspects of IPRs from a development perspective:

Some argue strongly that Intellectual Property Rights (IPRs) are necessary to stimulate economic growth, which, in turn, contributes to poverty reduction. By stimulating invention and new technologies, they will increase agricultural or industrial production, promote domestic and foreign investment, facilitate technology transfer and improve the availability of medicines necessary to combat disease ... .

Others argue equally vehemently the opposite. Intellectual Property rights do little to stimulate invention in developing countries, because the necessary human and technical capacity may be absent. They are ineffective at stimulating research to benefit poor people because they will not be able to afford the products, even if developed. They limit the option of technological learning through imitation. They allow foreign firms to drive out domestic competition by obtaining patent protection and to service the market through imports, rather than domestic manufacture. Moreover, they increase the costs of essential medicines and agricultural inputs, affecting poor people and farmers particularly badly.

[However] it is essential to consider the diversity of developing countries in respect of their social and economic circumstances and technological capabilities ... .

The determinants of poverty, and therefore the appropriate policies to address it, will vary accordingly between countries. The same applies to policies on IPRs. Policies required in countries with a relatively advanced technological capability where most poor people happen to live, for instance India or China, may well differ from those in other countries with a weak capability, such as many countries in sub-Saharan Africa. The impact of IP policies on poor people will also vary according to socio-economic circumstances. (Commission on Intellectual Property Rights, 2002, pp. 1–2)

Concluding remarks

The conceptual framework advanced in the first chapter of this book, the historical overview and the characterization of the 'triple crisis' of the second chapter, the examination of knowledge explosion and its manifestations in the third chapter, the characterization of the knowledge divide and its meaning for developing countries in Chapter 4, and the review of the emerging international context, of the experience with science and technology policies, and of strategies, policy instruments and international cooperation in Chapter 5, all point to the critical role that endogenous science and technology capabilities play in the process of development – whatever meaning may be given to this word – at the beginning of the 21st century.

Sir Francis Bacon's 1597 dictum *Nam et ipsa scientia potestas est* (knowledge itself is power) has become ever more accurate during the last few decades with the emergence of the knowledge society. It has also acquired ominous overtones as the huge disparities in science and technology capacities between rich and poor nations continue to deepen. Yet, determined action, backed by well-designed strategies, policies and international cooperation, could overcome this situation and make scientific and technological knowledge work for development.

Attempts to build endogenous science and technology capabilities at the beginning of the 21st century will take place in the context of a fractured global order. This constitutes a turbulent and uncertain setting for development, in which a variety of contradictory processes open up a wide range of opportunities and threats that defy established habits of thought. Among the fractures of this paradoxical world order, the knowledge divide is clearly the most important because of its pervasive and long-term consequences.

The key challenge faced by the international community in the 21st century is to prevent the multiplicity of fractures of the emerging global order from creating self-contained and partially isolated pockets of mutually distrustful peoples, ignorant and suspicious of the viewpoints, aspirations, potentials and capabilities of each other. It is essential to prevent these fractures from creating inward looking societies – a few of them with an endogenous science and technology base and most with extremely limited and disarticulated science, technology and innovation capabilities – that relate to one another only through tenuous symbolic links forged by mass media, or through narrowly circumscribed economic transactions.

The progressive establishment of an endogenous scientific and technological base in the developing countries need not follow necessarily the same path as that of the developed countries of today. In particular, there is a need to avoid the almost complete subordination of creativity and of knowledge generation to the logic of capital accumulation, which is primarily geared to and driven by the expansion of the production system and the search for profits. There must be room left for exploring alternative forces to drive the process of knowledge generation, and for integrating the achievements of modern science and technology with the cultural and knowledge heritage of non-Western societies. This would contribute to the emergence of distinct, pluralistic, integrated and continuously unfolding cultural identities in the developing world, a prerequisite for the self-confidence and self-esteem that underpin all development efforts.

These observations and the discussions in the preceding chapters of this book suggest four areas for additional research and study. These would shed light on the options available for developing countries to create endogenous science and technology capabilities, for bridging the knowledge divide and for exploring alternative avenues and meanings for the process of development. These four areas can be briefly summarized as follows:

- First, a broad and long-term program of comparative research and studies to explore the roles of knowledge and of values in different cultural settings, and how to evolve widely shared reinterpretations of the concepts of progress and development. The program should foster the exchange of views between civilizations and cultures, and include both developed and developing countries with different levels of science and technology capabilities.

- Second, a thorough examination of the evolution of the Baconian program, the reasons for its success and maturation, and of the challenges that it is facing in the early 21st century. This study should explore the outlines of possible alternative programs as humanity enters into the post-Baconian age, taking into consideration the potential contributions of non-Western cultures.

- Third, a comparative review and evaluation of strategies, policies and policy instruments to develop science, technology and innovation capabilities in different types of developing countries. The idea is to identify best practices and to gather information to assist policy- and decision-makers in the design of effective interventions to create an endogenous science and technology base.

- Fourth, the establishment of a task force to design the proposed global knowledge and development facility. This task force should involve representatives from governments, international institutions, private corporations, universities and research centers, scientific and professional societies and civil society organizations. In addition to designing the facility, this task force should conduct initial consultations with policy- and decision-makers to assess the feasibility of the proposals.

Private foundations and independent development cooperation agencies could play an especially important role in supporting these four areas of further study and research. In contrast with international financial institutions, which must be rather conservative to preserve their financial standing, and with bilateral cooperation agencies, which are instruments of foreign policy, private foundations and independent development cooperation agencies can take greater risks, choose more freely their areas of interest, engage more readily in joint programs, support initiatives for relatively long periods without having to show immediate results and operate in a flexible way without excessive administrative or political constraints. They are uniquely placed to undertake initiatives to face the Sisyphean challenge of building science and technology capabilities in developing countries, and to mobilize knowledge and innovation to improve the human condition.

Appendix 1   Comparison between the
              Science and Technology
              Capacity Index and other
              indexes (Technological
              Achievement Index of the
              Human Development Report,
              the RAND Index and the
              UNESCO Classification)

Appendix 1

Table A1.1 *Comparison between the categories of countries defined in the Science and Technology (S&T) Capacity Index and other indexes*

S&T Capacity Index	Technological Achievement Index	RAND Index	UNESCO
Type I	Leaders	Scientifically advanced countries	Industrialized countries with effective S&T bases
These countries have well-developed endogenous scientific and technological capacities and consolidated national system of innovation. Government policies encourage innovation and support the generation, acquisition and effective utilization of knowledge.	This group is at the cutting edge of technological innovation. Technological innovation is self-sustaining, and these countries have high achievements in technology creation, diffusion and skills.	These countries have greater S&T capacity than the international mean and higher capacity in all major areas of S&T. For example, they are responsible for 86% of all scientific articles published, and they fund between almost 90% of all the world's R&D.	These countries have greater S&T capacity than the international mean and higher capacity in all major areas of S&T. These countries are considered industrialized countries with effective S&T bases.
Type II	Potential leaders	Scientifically proficient countries	Countries with diversified S&T bases
These countries have relatively modest levels of endogenous scientific and technological capacities, usually focused on a few dynamic sectors of their economies. Even though most of them have well-developed human resources, they have not been able to create a broad base of scientific research and technological innovation activities that are linked to their production and service systems.	Most of these countries have invested in high levels of human skills and have diffused old technologies widely but innovate little. Each tends to rank low in one or two dimensions, such as diffusion of recent innovations or of old inventions. Most countries in this group have skill levels comparable to those in the top group.	These countries possess an overall S&T capacity index value at or over the international average, but they are not as uniformly capable as the advanced nations. Values for some capacity components may exceed the international average, while others may fall below the mean. Some of these countries display world-class strength in particular areas or subfields of science.	The countries and regions in this group have established an industrial basis, with a higher percentage of potential S&T manpower, and relatively high GDP per capita.

Table A1.1   continued

S&T Capacity Index	Technological Achievement Index	RAND Index	UNESCO
Government policies are mostly focused on the creation of science and technology capacities, but not necessarily geared to promote their integration with the production system.		These countries have made investments in the infrastructure and R&D required to build a science base, and these investments are showing results.	
Type III	Dynamic adopters	Scientifically developing countries	Countries with growing S&T bases
These countries are still in the early stages of establishing modern production systems and have very limited human resources, research and innovation capacities. Many have a few enclaves of modern production activities (often associated with foreign investment) coexisting with large areas of outmoded and obsolete production sectors. They face serious information, institutional and financial problems and government policies are not focused on the creation of capacities to generate, adapt, absorb and utilize knowledge.	These countries are dynamic in the use of new technology. Most are developing countries with significantly higher human skills than the fourth group. Many of these countries have important high-technology industries and technology hubs, but the diffusion of old inventions is slow and incomplete.	Although these nations have made some positive investments, their overall scientific capacity is below the world average. The investments that have been made, however, do allow these countries to participate in international S&T. These countries are seeking to invest further in science and, in some cases, they have good capabilities, which attract international partners. Several factors such as overall GNP or other infrastructural factors are keeping these countries from being considered among the above category.	These countries and regions are still in the process of industrialization. They have established a certain industrial basis, with moderate GDP per capita (upper-middle income and lower-middle income countries). Some have a relatively high percentage of potential S&T workers, but the potential is low in absolute terms.

Table A1.1   continued

S&T Capacity Index	Technological Achievement Index	RAND Index	UNESCO
Type IV	Marginalized	Scientifically lagging countries	Countries lacking an S&T base
These countries have practically no significant scientific research, technological development or innovation capacities, and also have a very limited S&T manpower base. Apart from the extraction of natural resources or the provision of some services (for example, offshore banking), which takes place in isolated enclaves, they generally use traditional technologies and some obsolete modern technologies, which operate at low levels of productivity and efficiency. Government policies pay little attention to science, technology and innovation issues.	Technology diffusion and skill building have a long way to go in these countries. Large parts of the population have not benefited from the diffusion of old technology.	These countries fall below the international mean for all the components of the S&T capacity index. In many cases, these countries have little or no capacity to conduct international level science. In other cases, scientific capacity that does exist has resulted from a natural or geographical resource located in these countries. In other cases, problems with infectious disease, natural disasters, or pollution, mean that international partners are interested in helping these countries, but they often find little indigenous capacity to tap for collaborative projects.	These countries and regions are still in the initial stage of development with low GDP per capita, low S&T manpower, but potential and a low percentage share of industrial and manufacturing sectors in production.

Table A1.2 Science and Technology (S&T) Capacity Index vs Technological Achievement Index

Technological Achievement Index (TAI)

Science and Technology Capacity Index		Leaders	Potential leaders	Dynamic adopters	Marginalized
	Type I	• Japan • United States • Sweden • Germany • Finland • United Kingdom • Netherlands • France • Korea, Rep. • Israel • Canada • Australia • Singapore • Norway • Ireland • Belgium • Austria	• Italy		
	Type II	• New Zealand	• Spain • Malaysia • Hungary • China • Slovenia • Czech Rep. • Hong Kong • Slovak Rep. • Mexico • Croatia • Poland • Greece • Portugal • Argentina • Romania • Chile	• Brazil • Thailand	
	Type III		• Bulgaria • Costa Rica	• Philippines • Jamaica • Iran • Egypt • Colombia • Peru • Indonesia • Panama • Tunisia	• Pakistan
	Type IV			• Ecuador • Syrian Arab Republic	
	Countries not considered by the S&T Capacity Index		• Cyprus	• Algeria • Bolivia • Dominican Republic • El Salvador • Honduras • Paraguay • Sri Lanka • Trinidad and Tobago • Uruguay • Zimbabwe	• Ghana • Kenya • Mozambique • Nepal • Nicaragua • Senegal • Sudan • Tanzania

Table A1.3 *Science and Technology (S&T) Capacity Index vs RAND Index*

		RAND			
S&T Capacity Index		Scientifically advanced countries	Scientifically proficient countries	Scientifically developing countries	Scientifically lagging countries
	Type I	• Japan • United States • Sweden • Germany • Finland • United Kingdom • Netherlands • France • Korea. Rep. • Israel • Canada • Australia • Norway • Ireland • Belgium • Denmark • Austria • Italy	• Singapore		
	Type II	• Russian Federation	• Ukraine • New Zealand • Spain • Hungary • China • Slovenia • Belarus • Czech Republic • Slovak Republic • South Africa • Croatia • Poland • Brazil • India • Greece • Cuba • Portugal • Estonia • Romania	• Hong Kong, China • Mexico • Argentina • Chile	• Malaysia
	Type III		• Bulgaria • Lithuania	• Turkey • Yugoslavia • Latvia • Venezuela • Iran • Egypt • Colombia • Philippines	• Jamaica • Peru • Costa Rica • Nigeria • Panama • Tunisia • Vietnam • Bangladesh
	Type IV			• Benin • Mauritius	• Ecuador • Kyrgyz Republic • Syrian Arab Republic • Burkina Faso • Central African Rep. • Congo. Rep. • Rwanda

Countries not considered by the S&T Capacity Index

- Luxembourg

- Armenia
- Bolivia
- Kuwait

- Macedonia
- Uzbekistan

- Albania
- Algeria
- Angola
- Botswana
- Cambodia
- Cameroon
- Congo
- Côte d'Ivoire
- Chad
- Dominican Republic
- El Salvador
- Eritrea
- Ethiopia
- Gabon
- Gambia
- Ghana
- Guinea
- Haiti
- Honduras
- Iraq
- Kenya
- Korea
- Lao PDR
- Lesotho
- Malawi
- Mali

- Mauritania
- Morocco
- Mozambique
- Myanmar
- Namibia
- Nepal
- Nicaragua
- Nigeria
- Oman
- Paraguay
- Saudi Arabia
- Senegal
- Sierra Leon
- Sri Lanka
- Sudan
- Tajikistan
- Tanzania
- Togo
- Trinidad and Tobago
- Uganda
- United Arab Emirates
- Uruguay
- Yemen
- Zambia
- Zimbabwe

Table A1.4 Science and Technology (S&T) Capacity Index vs UNESCO Index

S&T Capacity Index		UNESCO			
		Industrialized countries with effective S&T bases	Countries with diversified S&T bases	Countries with growing S&T bases	Countries lacking an S&T base
	Type I	• Japan • United States • Sweden • Germany • Finland • United Kingdom • Netherlands • France • Switzerland • Canada • Australia • Norway • Ireland • Belgium • Denmark • Austria • Italy	• Korea, Rep. • Israel • Singapore		• South Africa
	Type II	• Spain • Hungary • Poland	• New Zealand • Hong Kong, China • Mexico • Brazil • India • Greece • Cuba • Portugal • Argentina • Thailand • Chile	• Malaysia • China	
	Type III	• Bulgaria • Yugoslavia	• Turkey • Philippines • Venezuela • Egypt • Pakistan • Colombia • Peru • Costa Rica • Jordan • Panama • Guatemala • Vietnam	• Jamaica • Iran, Islamic Rep. • Indonesia • Nigeria • Tunisia	• Bangladesh
	Type IV		• Libya • Ecuador • Mauritius • Congo	• Mongolia • Gabon • Rwanda	• Benin • Burundi • Burkina Faso • Central African Rep. • Madagascar

Countries not considered by the S&T Capacity Index

- Czechoslovakia
- Germany DDR
- Germany FRG
- USSR

- Congo
- El Salvador
- Guyana
- Iceland
- Kuwait
- Lebanon
- Nicaragua
- Qatar
- Samoa
- Seychelles
- Sudan
- Trinidad and Tobago
- Uruguay

- Afghanistan
- Algeria
- Bahrain
- Barbados
- Bolivia
- Brunei-Darussalam
- Cambodia
- Cyprus
- Dominican Rep.
- Fiji
- Gabon
- Ghana
- Guinea

- Iraq
- Kenya
- Korea (Dem.)
- Luxembourg
- Malawi
- Malta
- Paraguay
- Saudi Arabia
- Senegal
- Sri Lanka
- Togo
- United Arab Emirates
- Zambia

- Albania
- Angola
- Bahamas
- Belize
- Bhutan
- Botswana
- Burma
- Cameroon
- Capo Verde
- Chad
- Djibouti
- Dominica
- Equatorial Guinea
- Ethiopia
- Granada
- Guyana
- Haiti
- Honduras
- Ivory Coast
- Lao
- Lesotho
- Liberia

- Maldives
- Mali
- Mauritania
- Morocco
- Mozambique
- Namibia
- Nepal
- Niger
- Oman
- Papua-New Guinea
- Sierra Leon
- Solomon Isl.
- Somalia
- Surinam
- Swaziland
- Taiwan
- Timor
- Uganda
- Yemen
- Zaire
- Zimbabwe

Notes:

The UNIDO Industrial Development Report has developed a composite index to benchmark industrial performance and rank 86 countries according to it. The Competitive Industrial Performance (CIP) index is an attempt to measure national ability to produce manufactures competitively and it is composed by four variables:

1. *Manufacturing value added (MVA) per capita*. MVA would automatically capture the competitiveness of industrial activity if all production from all countries were fully and equally exposed to international competition – but it is not. Trade and other policies limit the exposure of domestic industry to international competition. So do natural barriers to trade, such as high transport costs, poor access to natural resources, differences in taste, legal and institutional variations and information gaps. Production for home markets (particularly in countries with large markets or with strong import substitution policies) faces less intense competition than production for export.

127

2. *Manufactured exports per capita.* The export measure indicates how competitive industrial activity is in one set of markets. It also captures another important aspect of industrial performance: the ability of national industry to keep pace with technological change, at least in exported products. Exports can be taken to demonstrate that producers are using competitive (modern) technologies. This is important because the technology measures below do not capture technological upgrading within broad product groups. The export indicator partially offsets this inability.

3. *Share of medium- and high-technology activities in MVA.* The higher the share of medium- and high-technology activities in MVA, the more technologically complex is the industrial structure of a country, and the more competitive is the country's industrial performance. High-tech activities also enjoy better growth prospects and they often have dynamic international production systems. Even so, structural change is not automatic or easy because of the slow, incremental and path-dependent nature of learning. Many low-technology and resource-based industries can also have bursts of rapid growth; activities within these industries can have high-technology segments. And industries can shift between technological categories over time. Still, the technological complexity measure offers insights into the ability of countries to sustain growth in the new global setting.

4. *Share of medium- and high-technology products in manufactured exports.* The share of medium- and high-technology products in manufactured exports is considered separate from the share in MVA, because in certain circumstances the two differ significantly. In large import-substituting developing economies, for example, the structure of MVA tends to be more complex than that of exports.

The values for each of the four variables are standardized for the sample to range from zero (worst performers) to one (best performers). The composite index is calculated as a simple average of the four standardized basic indicators and no weights are assigned.

A ranking of economies by the CIP index reveals a general pattern that is as expected: industrialized countries congregate near the top, transition economies and middle-income developing countries around the middle, low-income developing countries and least developed countries at the bottom. Nonetheless, these results cannot be compared with those obtained with the S&T Capacity Index because the UNIDO report does not classify countries into categories.

Sources: International Council for Science Policy Studies (1990); UNDP (2001); UNIDO (2002); Wagner et al. (2001).

Appendix 2   Science, technology and development: the imperative of social innovation

A declaration issued by the former chairmen and members of the United Nations Advisory Committee on Science and Technology for Development (ACSTD) on the occasion of the tenth anniversary of the Vienna Programme of Action in October 1989

1. Humanity approaches a new century confronting a fundamental para-
    dox: we have never had so much power to influence the course of
    civilization, to shape the way our species will evolve, and to create an
    ever-expanding range of opportunities for human betterment – but we
    remain unwilling or unable to use this new-found power to achieve our
    full potential as human beings.
2. Throughout most of history, nations and societies have been compelled
    to behave as though some groups could only progress at the expense of
    others. Today, advances in science and technology have created new
    possibilities for all humanity to prosper, if we could but summon the
    collective will and wisdom to employ the new means available to us.
3. Science has been the most important factor in placing this unprec-
    edented opportunity within our grasp. During the past four centuries,
    the systematic process of subjecting abstract conceptions and proposi-
    tions about the world to the test of empirical observations – which is the
    hallmark of modern science – has superseded other forms of knowledge
    generation. As a result, science-based technologies are steadily replac-
    ing or improving those that developed through trial and error. At the
    same time, our understanding of the potentials and limitations of mod-
    ern science and its applications has increased considerably.
4. Paradoxically, progress in material well-being for a growing fraction of
    the world's population coexists with stagnation and even deterioration
    in standards of living for the majority of poor people. Deprivation of
    food, health, education and gainful employment besets a sizeable part
    of humanity, giving rise to new stresses on the environment which, in
    turn, undermine the basis for future development. The clash between

rising aspirations and the realities of omnipresent poverty, largely triggered by growing awareness of the life styles of the affluent, has become a source of social tension, intolerance and violence.

5. The now enormous potential for human advancement coexists with gross inequalities, possible ominous threats to the global commons (such as the greenhouse effect and stratospheric ozone depletion), and with the diversion of a significant proportion of the world's highest intellectual talent to develop technologies so awesome as to threaten human survival. This paradox puts in sharp relief the critical problem of our age: our scientific knowledge and technological mastery have outstripped our collective capacity to manage advances in science and technology so as to enhance the opportunities and reduce the threats they create. A bold and imaginative effort in social and institutional innovation at all levels from local to international – is now essential for survival and progress.

6. The 1980s have been through many changes and surprises: the reversal of capital flows between North and South as a consequence of the debt crisis, the information revolution and proliferation of personal computers, significant advances in biotechnology, the tragic emergence of AIDS pandemic, the explosive growth of megacities in the third world, and a major redistribution of economic world power, among many others. A new and as yet fluid world order has been in the making in the decade since the United Nations Conference on Science and Technology for Development was held at Vienna in 1979.

7. In this rapidly evolving global context, the 1990s may offer historic opportunities for broader international cooperation in science and technology. After four decades of antagonism and mistrust, the bipolar divisions of the world – East/West and North/South – are giving way to a pluralistic international environment. This creates a unique opportunity for more equitable and pragmatic distribution of the costs and benefits of scientific and technological progress, casting aside the ideological blinders that constrained the visions of statesmen for nearly half a century. Our enormous and increasing stock of scientific knowledge and technological skills can become a key resource for easing international tensions.

8. We propose three guiding principles for a renewed mobilization of science and technology in the service of development. The international community of statesmen, scientists, policy-makers, scholars, professionals, managers, workers and citizens – within which the United Nations system should play a leading role – must in our view:

   (a) Evolve a broad new strategy to ensure equality of access for all people to modern scientific and technological knowledge essential to alleviating poverty, reducing population pressures, achieving minimum standards of health and nutrition, improving educational opportunities, and promoting economic growth. Without sacrificing the incentives for individual creativity and practical imagination, we must evolve a common view that scientific and technological progress should directly foster global equity, both within and between generations;

(b) Undertake a concerted effort to build the human and institutional capacities developing countries need to make independent decisions on the critical science and technology issues which will confront them. International cooperation will play a mayor role in this essential task, particularly because of the huge disparities in scientific and technological capabilities between the industrialized and the developing countries – disparities that dwarf other indicators of global inequality;

(c) Forge new international partnerships to achieve environmentally sustainable development. The times when humanity could act on the physical and biological environment with impunity – blindly trusting in the regenerative powers of ecosystems – are forever gone. New approaches in which humanity and nature jointly enhance each other's capacities are imperative. This will demand a re-evaluation of the many ways in which different cultures relate to the natural world, using science to build constructively on this diversity, rather than seeking to universalize some single over-arching view of the interactions between human activities and the environment.

9. We believe a successful collective search for social innovations during the last decade of the twentieth century will require a climate of openness and participation at all levels. Imposed solutions or visions – however well conceived – will lack authority in today's increasingly pluralistic political communities. Tolerance for cultural and religious diversity, respect for human rights, active encouragement of individual freedom and creativity, and sensitivity to the damaging effects of inequalities of knowledge and power are essential for linking science and technology to the preservation and advancement of humanity.

10. We reaffirm our belief in international cooperation as the most effective way to transcend the conditions which deny the power and benefits of science and technology to those most in need. International cooperation and assistance must evolve beyond charity, or narrowly conceived national interest, into expressions of collective responsibility for the well-being of all humanity in present and future generations.

11. We strongly encourage the international community to develop during the next decade a multiplicity of innovative approaches to bilateral,

regional and global cooperation in science and technology for development. The United Nations should monitor these initiatives, fostering the exchange of experiences, and when this century comes to an end, 20 years after the 1979 Vienna Conference, should arrange an international gathering to evaluate progress and chart the course for science and technology for development in the new century.

Francisco Sagasti (Peru), Chairman 1988–89
Essam El-din Galal (Egypt), Chairman 1986–87
Umberto Colombo (Italy), Chairman 1984–85
M.S. Swaminathan (India), Chairman 1981–83

(The signature of the other 45 Committee members follows.)

Bibliography

This bibliography contains material that has been directly consulted in the preparation of this book, even when it has not been quoted in the text. The articles, papers, monographs and books written by the author and mentioned in this bibliography contain additional references that provided inputs to this book in an indirect way.

Alvares, Claude (1979), *Homo Faber: Technology and Culture in India, China and the West 1500 to the Present Day*, New Delhi: Allied.

Amsden, Alice H., Ted Tschang and Akira Goto (2001), 'Do foreign companies conduct R&D in developing countries? A new approach to analyzing the level of R&D, with an analysis of Singapore', Tokyo, Asian Development Bank Institute, Working Paper No. 14.

Andersen, Esben and Morris Teubal (1999), 'High tech cluster creation and cluster re-configuration – a systems and policy perspective', Hebrew University, Jerusalem, and Jerusalem Institute for Israel Studies, papers for the DRUID Conference on National Innovation Systems, June.

Annerstedt, Jan (1994), 'Measuring science, technology and innovation', in J.J. Salomon, F. Sagasti and C. Sachs-Jeantet (eds), *The Uncertain Quest: Science, Technology and Development*, Tokyo: United Nations University Press, pp. 96–125.

Aráoz, Alberto and Francisco Sagasti (1979), 'The outlook for science and technology planning in developing countries', in F. Sagasti and A. Aráoz (eds), *Science and Technology for Development: Planning in the STPI Countries*, Ottawa: International Development Research Centre, pp. 9–20.

Arocena, Rodrigo and Judith Sutz (2000), 'Looking at national systems of innovation from the South', *Industry and Innovation*, 7 (1), 55–75.

Arocena, Rodrigo and Judith Sutz (2001a), 'Revisiting Nelson and Winter from the South: "Learning by Solving" in underdeveloped countries', paper submitted to the Druid's Summer Conference.

Arocena, Rodrigo and Judith Sutz (2001b), 'Changing knowledge production and Latin American universities', *Research Policy* , **30**, 1221–34.

Arocena, Rodrigo and Judith Sutz (2001c), 'Desigualdad, Tecnología e Innovación en el Desarrollo Latinoamericano', *Iberoamericana* , **I** (1), 29–49.

Arocena, Rodrigo and Judith Sutz (2001d), 'Valores, Intereses Privados y Agendas de Investigación Universitarias: Una Mirada Desde el Sur', in A.A. Cellino (ed.), *Los Laberintos del Futuro: Ciencia y Técnica: Perspectivas y Desafíos en América Latina*, Santa Fe, Argentina: Centro de Publicaciones de la Universidad Nacional del Litoral.

Ayala, Francisco J. (1996), 'Introductory essay: the case for scientific literacy', in UNESCO, *World Science Report 1996*, Paris: UNESCO.

Bacon, Francis ([1627] 1985), *The Essays*, edited with an introduction by John Pitcher, London: Penguin Books.

Banco Interamericano de Desarrollo (BID) (2001), *Competitividad: el motor del crecimiento, Progreso Económico y Social en América Latina: Informe 2001*, Washington, DC: Banco Interamericano de Desarrollo.

Barloewen, Constantin von (1995), *History and Modernity in Latin America: Technology and Culture in the Andes Region*, Providence, RI: Berghahn Books.

Barnett, Andrew (1994), 'Knowledge transfer and developing countries: the tasks for science and technology in the global perspective 2010', *Science and Public Policy*, **21** (1), 2–12.

Barret, William (1979), *The Illusion of Technique*, New York: Doubleday.

Basalla, George (1967), 'The spread of Western science', *Science*, **156**, 611–22.

Ben-David, Joseph (1972), *The Scientists' Role in Society*, Englewood Cliffs, NJ: Prentice-Hall.

Berger, Peter, Brigitte Berger and Hansfield Keller (1974), *The Homeless Mind: Modernization and Consciousness*, Harmondsworth: Penguin.

Berlinguet, L. (1978), 'Views on the transfer of technology based on recent programmes in the third world', presented at the OECD seminar on 'Science and Technology Policies and Activities of Member Governments to Meet the Needs of Developing Countries', Paris, 10–13 April.

Berman, Morris (1981), *The Reenchantment of the World*, Ithaca, NY: Cornell University Press.

Bernal, J. (1971), *Science in History*, Cambridge, MA: MIT Press.

Bernal, J.D. ([1937] 1967), *The Social Function of Science*, Cambridge, MA: MIT Press.

Bezanson, K., J. Annerstedt, K. Chung, D. Hopper, G. Oldham and F. Sagasti (1999), *Viet Nam at the Crossroads: The Role of Science and Technology*, Ottawa: International Development Research Centre.

Bezanson, Keith A. and Geoffrey Oldham (2000), 'Issues and options concerning a European foundation for research for development', Brighton, Institute of Development Studies.

Bezanson, Keith, Francisco Sagasti and collaborators (2000), *A Foresight and Policy Study of the Multilateral Development Banks*, Stockholm: Ministry for Foreign Affairs of Sweden.

Bhalla, Agit (1993), 'Technology choice and development,' in J.-J. Salomon, F. Sagasti and C. Sachs (eds), *The Uncertain Quest: Science, Technology and Development*, Tokyo: United Nations University Press.

Bhalla, Agit and Dilmus James (eds) (1988), *New Technologies and Development: Experiences with Technology Blending*, Boulder, CO: Lynne Rienner.

Bhalla, Agit, Dilmus D. James and Y. Stevens (1984), *Blending of New and Traditional Technologies: Case Studies*, Dublin: Tycooly International.

Blumentritt, Rolf and Ron Johnston (1999), 'Towards a strategy for knowledge management', *Technology Analysis & Strategic Management*, **11** (3), 287–300.

Bok, Sissela (1995), *Common Values*, Columbia, MO: Columbia University of Missouri Press.

Braudel, Fernand (1975), *Las Civilizaciones Actuales*, Madrid: Editorial Tecnos.

Brockman, John (2002), *The Next Fifty Years: Science in the First Half of the Twenty-First Century*, New York: Vintage Books.

Bronowski, Jacob (1965), *Science and Human Values*, New York: Harper Torchbooks.

Camus, Albert (1942), *Le Myth de Sisyphes*, Paris: Gallimard (translation Justin O'Brien (1955), *The Myth of Sisyphus*, London: Hamish Hamilton, p. 96).

Carlsson, Bo, Staffan Jacobsson, Magnus Holmén and Annika Rickne (2002),

'Innovation systems: analytical and methodological issues', *Research Policy*, **31**, 233–45.

Carnegie Commission on Science, Technology and Government (1992), *Partnerships for Global Development: The Clearing Horizon*, New York: Carnegie Corporation.

Castro, Claudio de Moura, Laurence Wolf and John Alic (2001), 'Science and technology for development: an IDB strategy', Washington, DC, Inter-American Development Bank, Sustainable Development Department.

Choucri, Nazli (1998), 'Knowledge networking for technology "Leapfrogging"', *Co-operation South*, (2), 40–52.

Chung, KunMo (1977), *Technology and Industrial Development in Korea*, final report, Korean STPI Project, Seoul: Korean Advanced Institute of Sciences.

Cleveland, Harlan, Garry Jacobs, Robert Macfarlane, Robert van Harten and N. Asokan (1999), *Human Choice: The Genetic Code for Social Development*, San Francisco, CA: World Academy of Arts and Sciences.

Cohen, Benjamin R. (2001), 'Science and humanities: across two cultures and into science studies', *Endeavour*, **25** (1), 8–12.

Collantes, Carlos (1975), *Perspectives d'Ecodeveloppement pour L'Amazonie Peruvienne*, Paris: Centre International de Recherche sur l'Environment et le Developpement.

Commission on Intellectual Property Rights (2002), *Integrating Intellectual Property Rights with Development Policy*, London: United Kingdom Department for International Development.

Cooper, Charles (1984), 'Strengthening of scientific and technological capacities for industrial development in developing countries,' Vienna, background paper for the Fourth General Conference of UNIDO, 2–18, August, doc. no. ID/CONF.6/6.

Cooper, Charles (1992), 'Are innovation studies on industrialized economies relevant to technology policy in developing countries?', Maastrich, United Nations University Institute for New Technologies (UNU/INTECH).

Coriat, Benjamin and Olivier Weinstein (2002), 'Organizations, firms and institutions in the generation of innovation', *Research Policy*, **31**, 273–90.

Dahlman, Carl (1994), 'The third industrial revolution: trends and implication for developing countries', paper prepared for Foro Nacional International Conference on the New International Order, Rio de Janeiro, Brazil, 13–14 April.

Daly, John (1997), 'Summary of the session on the role of foundations', World Bank conference on science and technology for development, Toronto, 23 June.

Davenport, Sally and David Bibby (1999), 'Rethinking a national innovation system: the small country as "SME"', *Technology Analysis & Strategic Management*, **11** (3), 431–62.

David, Paul and Dominique Foray (2002), 'Fundamentos Económicos de la Sociedad del Conocimiento', *Comercio Exterior*, **52** (6), 472–90.

de Riencourt, Amaury (1981), *The Eye of Shiva: Eastern Mysticism and Science*, New York: Morrow Quill Paperbacks.

De, Nitish (1977), 'Adaptation of traditional systems of agriculture in a developing economy', Occasional Papers Series No. 2, National Labour Institute, New Delhi.

Dean, Genevieve (1976), 'Technology and industrialization in the People's Republic of China, office of the field coordinator', Lima, STPI Project, July.

Desai, Megnad, Sakiko Fukuda-Parr, Carl Johansson and Francisco Sagasti (2001), 'A new map of technology creation and diffusion – measuring technology achievement of nations and the capacity to participate in the network age', New York: United Nations Development Programme, Human Development Report Office.

Development Cooperation (2000), Special issue on 'Designing the future: South South cooperation in science and technology', *Development Cooperation*, (1), 4–89.

Drucker, Peter (1968), *The Age of Discontinuity*, New York: Harper and Row.

Drucker, Peter (1994), 'The age of social transformation', *Atlantic Monthly*, November, 53–80.

Drucker, Peter (1999), 'Beyond the information revolution', *Atlantic Monthly*, October, 47–57.

Economist, The (1988), 'The other group of seven', *The Economist*, 4 June, pp. 73–4.

Economist, The (1996), 'Roll your own: scientific instruments', *The Economist*, 3 February, pp. 71–2.

Einstein, Albert (1954), *Ideas and Opinions*, New York: Wings Books.

Elkana, Yehuda (1977), 'The distinctiveness and universality of science: reflections on the work of Professor Robin Horton', *Minerva*, **15** (2), 155–73.

Ellul, Jacques (1980), *The Technological System*, New York: Continuum.

Emery, Fred and Eric Trist (1973), *Towards a Social Ecology: Contextual Appreciations of the Future in the Present*, London: Plenum Press.

Ernst, Dieter and David O'Connor (1989), *Technology and Global Competition: The Challenge for the Newly Industrialized Economies*, Paris: Organization for Economic Cooperation and Development Development Center.

Ernst, Dieter, Tom Ganiatsos and Lynn Mytelka (eds) (1998), *Technological Capabilities and Export Success in Asia*, London: Routledge.

Fernández-Armesto, Felipe (1995), *Millennium: A History of the Last Thousand Years*, New York: Touchstone.

Flit, Isaías (1977), 'La Investigación Tecnológica y el Desarrollo Industrial', Lima: INTINTEC.

Flores, Gustavo (1975), 'Contribución del INTINTEC al Desarrollo de una Capacidad Tecnológica Nacional', in INTINTEC, *La Investigación Tecnológica Industrial en el Perú*, Lima: INTINTEC.

Frazer, James (1964), *The New Golden Bough*, New York: Mentor Books.

Freeman, C. (ed.) (1983), *Long Waves in the World Economy*, London: Butterworth.

Freeman, Chris (2002), 'Continental, national and sub-national innovation systems – complementarity and economic growth', *Research Policy*, **31**, 191–211.

Freeman, C. and J. Hagedoorn (1992), 'Globalization of technology: global perspective 2010 and the tasks for science and technology', Brighton: Science Policy Research Unit, University of Sussex.

Freeman, Christopher and Carlota Pérez (1988), 'Structural cycles of adjustment, business cycles and investment behavior,' in G. Dosi, C. Freeman, R.R. Nelson, G. Silverberg and L. Soete (eds), *Technical Change and Economic Theory*, London: Frances Pinter.

Friedman, Andrew L. (1999), 'Rhythm and evolution of information technology', *Technology Analysis and Strategic Management*, **11** (3), 375–90.

Furtado, Celso (1962), *Desarrollo y Subdesarrollo*, Buenos Aires: Editorial Universitaria de Buenos Aires.

Furtado, Celso (1970), *Obstacles to Development in Latin America*, New York: Anchor Books.

Furtado, Celso (1979), *Creatividad y Dependencia*, México DF: Siglo XXI Editores.

Gaillard, Jacques (1994), 'The behaviour of scientists and scientific communities,' in J.J. Salomon, F. Sagasti and C. Sachs-Jeantet (eds), *The Uncertain Quest: Science, Technology, and Development*, Tokyo: United Nations University Press.

Gallopin, Guilberto (2001), 'Science and technology, sustainability and sustainable development', Santiago de Chile: Economic Commission for Latin America and the Caribbean.

Garaudy, Roger (1981), 'Notes for a keynote search at the Fifth Parliamentary and Scientific Conference of the Council of Europe', Helsinki, June.

García Morente, Manuel ([1933] 1980), *Ensayos sobre el Progreso*, Madrid: Editorial Dorcas.

General Agreement on Trade and Tariffs (now World Trade Organization) (2002), 'Trade liberalization statistics', http://www.gatt.org/trastat_e.html

Girvan, Norman (1984), *Technology Policies for Small Developing Economies: A Study of the Caribbean*, Ottawa: International Development Research Centre.

Goonatilake, Susantha (1984), *Aborted Discovery: Science and Creativity in the Third World*, London: Zed Press.

Goulet, Dennis (1977), *The Uncertain Promise: Value Conflicts in Technology Transfer*, Washington, DC: Overseas Development Council.

Groupe de Lisbonne (1995), *Limites à la Compétitivité: Pour Un Nouveau Contrat Mondial*, Paris: La Decouverte.

Guilder, George (2000), *Telescom: How Infinite Bandwidth Will Revolutionize Our World*, New York: Free Press.

Gusdorf, G. and Tarascio V.J. (1972), 'Development: the concept and its career in economics', in C.A.O. Van Nieuwenhuijze (ed.), *Development: The Western View*, The Hague: Mouton.

Halty-Carrère, Máximo (1975), 'Towards a new technology order?', paper presented at the OECD seminar on Science, Technology and Development in a Changing World, Paris, April.

Halty-Carrère, Máximo (1986), *Estrategias de Desarrollo Tecnológico para Países en Desarrollo*, México DF: El Colegio de México

Hanna, Nagy (1991), 'Informatics and the developing world', *Finance and Development*, **28** (4), 45–8.

Hariharan, Venkaresh (1999), 'Owning knowledge, owning the future', *Information Technology in Developing Countries*, **9** (3), 11–12.

Hassan, Mohamed H.A. (2000), 'Challenges, opportunities and strategies for South–South cooperation in science and technology in the 21st century', in A. Rath and S. Lealess (eds), *Technology for People: Forum on South–South Cooperation in Science and Technology (FOSAT)*, Ottawa: Policy Research International Inc.

Hawking, Stephen (1993), *Black Holes and Baby Universes,* New York: Bantam Books.

Heim, Michael (1993), *The Metaphysics of Virtual Reality*, Oxford: Oxford University Press.

Heisenberg, Werner (1958), *Physics and Philosophy*, New York: Harper Torchbooks.

Herman, Robert, S.A. Ardekani and Jesse Ausubel (1989), 'Dematerialization', in J.H. Ausubel and H.E. Sladovich (eds), *Technology and Environment*, Washington, DC: National Academy Press, pp. 50–69.

Herrera, Amílcar (1976), 'Scientific and traditional technologies in developing countries', Brighton, Science Policy Research Unit, Sussex University.

Herrera, Amílcar (1978), 'Research and development systems in rural settings: background to the project', México DF, Facultad Latinoamericana de Ciencias Sociales.

Hobsbawm, Eric (1994), *The Age of Extremes: A History of the World 1914–1991*, New York: Pantheon Books

Hoffman, Kurt (1989), 'Technological advance and organizational innovation in the engineering industry: a new perspective on problems and possibilities for the developing countries', Washington, DC, World Bank, Industry and Energy Department Working Paper No. 4.

Hopper, David (1973), *Research Policy: Eleven Issues*, Ottawa: International Development Research Centre.

Horgan, John (1996), *The End of Science: Facing the Limits of Knowledge in the Twilight of the Science Age*, New York: Broadway Books.

Hunt, Patrick (2000), 'Knowledge management: implications and applications for development organizations', report of a workshop co-organized by the Bellanet International Secretariat, the Benton Foundation, the Canadian International Development Agency, and the International Development Research Centre, Washington, DC, Benton Foundation, 2–4 February.

International Council for Science Policy Studies, (1990), *Science and Technology in Developing Countries: Strategies for the 90s: A Report to UNESCO*, Paris: UNESCO.

International Telecommunication Union (ITU) (2002), 'Recent trends in the Internet world: numbering cyberspace', Telecommunication Indicators Update January–February–March 2001, http://www.itu.int/ITU-D/ict/update/

Jaguaribe, Helio (1971), 'Ciencia y Tecnología en el Cuadro Socio Político de América Latina', *El Trimestre Económico*, (150), 389–432.

Jamison, Andrew (2001), 'Science and the quest for sustainable development', *Technological Analysis & Strategic Management*, **13** (1), 9–22.

Jardine, Lisa and Alan Stewart (1998), *Hostage to Fortune: The Troubled Life of Francis Bacon*, New York: Hill and Wang.

Jonas, Hans (1984), *The Imperative of Responsibility*, Chicago: Chicago University Press.

Jordan, Judith (1999), 'Constructing tomorrow: technology strategies for the next millennium', *Technology Analysis & Strategic Management*, **11** (3), 285–6.

Juma, Calestous and Victor Konde (2002), 'Technical change and sustainable development: developing country perspectives', Boston: Annual Meeting and Science Innovation Exposition, American Association for the Advancement of Science, 14–19 February.

Juma, Calestous, K. Fang, D. Honca, J. Hunte-Perez, V. Konde, S.H. Lee, J. Arenas, A. Ivinson, H. Robinson and S. Singh (2001), 'Global governance of technology: meeting the needs of developing countries', *International Journal of Technology Management*, **22** (7/8), 629–55.

Jupiter Comunications (2000), *Latin America: Online Projection*, New York: Jupiter Analyst Report.

Kaplinsky, Raphael (1984), *Automation: The Technology and Society*, Harlow: Longman.

Katz, Jorge (2000), 'Pasado y Presente del Comportamiento Tecnológico de América Latina', Serie Desarrollo Productivo No. 75, Santiago de Chile: Comisión Económica para América Latina y el Caribe de las Naciones Unidas.

Katz, Jorge (2001), *Structural Reforms, Productivity and Technological Change in Latin America*, Santiago de Chile: United Nations Economic Commission for Latin America and the Caribbean.

Katz, Jorge and Mario Cimoli (2002), 'Interdependencias entre lo Macro y Microeconómico, Cambio Tecnológico y Crecimiento Económico', Santiago de Chile: Comisión Económica para América Latina y el Caribe de las Naciones Unidas.

Katz, Jorge and Giovanni Stumpo (2001), 'Regímenes Competitivos Sectoriales, Productividad y Competitividad Internacional', Serie Desarrollo Productivo No. 103, Santiago de Chile, Comisión Económica para América Latina y el Caribe de las Naciones Unidas.

Kim, Linsu (1991), 'Technology policy for industrialization: an integrative framework and Korea's experience', *Research Policy*, **21**, 437–52.

Knudtson, Peter and David Suzuki (2001), *Wisdom of the Elders*, Toronto: Stoddart.

Kodama, Fumio (1995), *Emerging Patterns of Innovation: Sources of Japan's Technological Edge*, Cambridge, MA: Harvard Business School Press.

Konetzke, Richard (1972), *América Latina: La Época Colonial*, México DF: Siglo XXI Editores.

Kranzberg, Melvin (1989), 'The dynamic ecology of innovation,' in M. Kranzberg, Y. Elkana and Z. Tadmor (eds), *Innovation at the Crossroads Between Science and Technology*, Haifa: Neaman Press.

Kumar, Nagesh (1997), 'Technology generation and technology transfers in the world economy: recent trends and implications for developing countries', Maastricht: United Nations University Institute of New Technologies.

Kuramoto, Juana and Francisco Sagasti (2002), 'Integrating local and global knowledge, technology and production systems: challenges for technical cooperation', in S. Fukuda-Parr, C. Lopes and K. Malik (eds), *Capacity for Development: New Solutions to Old Problems*, London: Earthscan Publications.

Kuznets, Simon (1971), *Population, Capital and Growth*, New York: Norton.

Ladriere, Jean (1977), *El Reto de la Racionalidad: La Ciencia y la Tecnología Frente a las Culturas*, Madrid: Ediciones Sígueme.

Lall, Sanjaya (2000a), 'Turkish performance in exporting manufactures: a comparative structural analysis', Oxford: Oxford University, Queen Elizabeth House Working Paper Series No. 47.

Lall, Sanjaya (2000b), 'Skills, competitiveness and policy in developing countries', Oxford: Oxford University, Queen Elizabeth House Working Paper Series No. 46.

Lall, Sanjaya (2000c), 'The technological structure and performance of developing countries: manufactured exports, 1985–1998', Oxford: Oxford University, Queen Elizabeth House Working Paper Series No. 44.

Lall, Sanjaya (2001), 'Harnessing technology for human development', in UNDP, *Human Development Report 2001*, New York: United Nations Development Programme.

Lall, Sanjaya (2003), 'Industrial success and failure in a globalizing world', Oxford: Oxford University, Queen Elizabeth House Working Paper Series No. 102.

Lall, Sanjaya and Morris Teubal (1998), 'Market-stimulating technology policies in developing countries: a framework with examples from East Asia', *World Development*, **26** (8), 1369–85.

Landes, David (1969), *The Unbound Prometheus*, Cambridge: Cambridge University Press.

Linowes, David F. (1990), 'Speech delivered to the White House Conference on Libraries and Information Services, October 1990'; quoted by Carl Dahlman, 'The third industrial revolution: trends and implications for developing countries', paper presented at the Foro Nacional International Conference on the New International Order, Rio de Janeiro, Brazil, 13–14 April 1994.

Lundvall, Bengt-Åke, Björn Johnson, Esben Sloth Andersen and Bent Dalum (2002), 'National system of production, innovation and competence building', *Research Policy*, **31**, 213–31.

Machlup, Fritz (1962), *The Production and Distribution of Knowledge in the United States*, Princeton, NJ: Princeton University Press.

Machlup, Fritz (1980), *Knowledge: Its Creation, Distribution and Economic Significance, Volume 1: Knowledge and Knowledge Production*, Princeton, NJ: Princeton University Press.

Maddison, Angus (1995), *Monitoring The World Economy 1820–1992*, Paris: Organization for Economic Cooperation and Development, Development Centre.

Maddison, Angus (2001), *The World Economy: A Millennial Perspective*, Paris: Organization for Economic Cooperation and Development, Development Centre.

Malerba, Franco (2002), 'Sectoral systems of innovation and production', *Research Policy*, **31**, 247–64.

Malinowski, Bronislaw (1974), *Magia, Ciencia, Religión*, Barcelona: Editorial Ariel.

Mansell, Robin and Uta Wehn (1998), *Knowledge Societies: Information Technology for Sustainable Development*, a report to the United Nations Commission on Science and Technology for Development, Oxford: Oxford University Press.

Marx, Karl ([1867] 1976), *Das Capital*, vol. 1, Harmondsworth: Penguin Books.

Mehmet, Özay and Hasan Alı Biçak (2002), *Modern and Traditional Irrigation Technologies in the Eastern Mediterranean*, Ottawa: International Development Research Centre.

Mellov, Felicity (1999), 'Scientists' rhetoric in the science wars', *Public Understanding of Science*, **8**, 51–6.

Mendelssohn, Kurt (1976), *The Secret of Western Domination: How Science Became the Key to Global Power, and What this Signifies for the Rest of the World*, New York: Praeger.

Mendis, D.L.O. (1977), *Some Thoughts on Technology Transfer for Irrigation and Multi-Purpose in Sri Lanka*, Colombo: Transactions of the Institute of Engineers of Sri Lanka.

Montamedi, Beatrice (1993), 'Computer designed pharmaceuticals', *Hemispheres*, November, 51–2.

Moravcsik, Michael J. (1975), *Science Development: The Building of Science in Less Developed Countries*, Bloomington, IN: PASITAM.

Mowery, David and Nathan Rosemberg (1989), *Technology and the Pursuit of Economic Growth*, Cambridge: Cambridge University Press.

Mozley Roche, Edward (1997), 'Computer industry almanac: data on computer usage', *Information Technology in Developing Countries*, **7** (1), www.iimahd.ernet.in/egov/ifip/jan97.htm.

Mumford, Lewis (1970), *The Pentagon of Power: The Myth of the Machine*, New York: Harcourt Brace, Jovanovich.

Murra, J. (1975), *Formaciones Económicas y Políticas el Mundo Andino*, Lima: Instituto de Estudios Peruanos.

Musson, Alfred E. (ed.) (1972), *Science, Technology and Economic Growth in the 18th Century*, Cambridge: Cambridge University Press.

Mytelka, Lynn and John F.E. Ohiorhenuan (2000), 'South–South cooperation in knowledge-based industrial development', in A. Rath and S. Lealess (eds), *Technology for People: Forum on South–South Cooperation in Science and Technology (FOSAT)*, Ottawa: Policy Research International Inc.

Narayanan, K.R. (1987), *Images and Insights*, New Delhi: Allied.

Nasr, Seyyed Hossein (1970), *Science and Civilization in Islam*, New York: Plume Books.

Needham, Joseph (1977), *La Gran Titulación: Ciencia y Sociedad en Oriente y Occidente*, Madrid: Alianza Editorial.

Nelson, Benjamin (1981), *On the Roads to Modernity: Conscience, Science and Civilizations*, Totowa, NJ: Rowman and Littlefield.

Nelson, Richard (ed.) (1993), *National Innovation Systems: A Comparative Analysis*, Oxford: Oxford University Press.

Nelson, Richard R. and Katherine Nelson (2002), 'Technology, institutions, and innovation systems', *Research Policy*, **31**, 265–72.

Nerfin, Marc (1975), *Qué Hacer? Hacia Otro Desarrollo*, Uppsala: Fundación Dag Hammarskjold.

Nerfin, Marc (ed.) (1977), *Towards Another Development: Approaches and Strategies*, Uppsala: Dag Hammarskjöld Foundation.

Nerfin, Marc (1987), 'Neither prince nor merchant: citizen', *Development Dialogue*, (1), 170–95.

Niosi, Jorge (2002), 'National systems of innovation are 'X-efficient' (and X-effective): why some are slow learners', *Research Policy*, **31**, 291–302.

Nisbet, Robert (1980), *History of the Idea of Progress*, New York: Basic Books.

Noble, David (1977), *America by Design*, New York: Knopf.

Nye, Joseph S. Jr and William A. Owens (1996), 'America's information edge', *Foreign Affairs*, **75** (3–4), 20–36.

Oldham, Geoffrey (ed.) (1997), *A Decade of Reform: Science and Technology – Policy in China*, Ottawa: International Development Research Centre.

Olson, Theodore (1982), *Millennialism, Utopianism, and Progress*, Toronto: University of Toronto Press.

Organization for Economic Cooperation and Development (OECD) (1996), *OECD in Figures – Statistics on the Member Countries: 1996 Edition*, Paris: OECD.

Organization for Economic Cooperation and Development (OECD) (1998), *21st Century Technologies: Promises and Perils of a Dynamic Future*, Paris: OECD.

Organization for Economic Cooperation and Development (OECD) (1999), *Managing National Innovation Systems*, Paris: OECD.

Organization for Economic Cooperation and Development (OECD) (2000), '21st century governance: power in the global knowledge economy and society', Expo 2000–OECD Forum for the Future; Hanover, 25 and 26 March, Paris: OECD.

Ortega y Gasset, José ([1933]1968), *Meditación de la Técnica*, Madrid: El Arquero-Revista de Occidente.

Ozlak, A., M. Cavarozzi, and S. Sonino (1976), 'El INTI y el Desarrollo Industrial de Argentina, Buenos Aires', a report of the Argentinean STPI Project team.

Pacey, Arnold (1974), *The Maze of Ingenuity: Ideas and Idealism in the Development of Technology*, Cambridge, MA: MIT Press.

Pacey, Arnold (1983), *The Culture of Technology*, Cambridge, MA: MIT Press.

Park, Hokoon (2000), 'A new partnership for science and technology development: the roles of state, R&D institution and private sector', in A. Rath and S. Lealess (eds), *Technology for People: Forum on South–South Cooperation in Science and Technology (FOSAT)*, Ottawa: Policy Research International Inc.

Pérez, Carlota (1989), 'Technical change, competitive restructuring and institutional reform in developing countries', Discussion Paper No. 4, Strategic Planning and Review Department, Washington, DC: World Bank.

Pérez, Carlota (2001), 'Technological change and opportunities for development as a moving target', *ECLAC Review*, No. 75.

Pérez, Carlota (2002), *Technological Revolutions and Financial Capital*, Cheltenham, UK and Northampton, MA, USA: Edward Elgar.

Petrella, Ricardo (1983), 'Le Changement dans L'Environement Externe a la R&D: la Dimension Europeene,' Forecasting and Assessment of Technology (FAST) Occasional Paper No. 64, Brussels: European Union.

Pharma (2000), 'Why do prescription drugs cost so much and other questions about yours medicines', in www.phrma.org, Washington, DC, Pharmaceutical Research and Manufacturers of America Association.

Pitt, Martin and Ken Clerke (1999), 'Competing on competence: a knowledge perspective on the management of strategic innovation', *Technology Analysis & Strategic Management*, **11** (3), 301–16.

Polanyi, Karl (1957), *The Great Transformation*, Boston, MA: Beacon Press.

Prebisch, Raúl (1952), *Problemas Teóricos y Prácticos del Crecimiento Económico'*, Santiago de Chile: Comisión Económica para América Latina.

Pyramid Research (1999), 'Will the Internet close the gap?', report prepared for the InfoDev program, Washington, DC: World Bank.

Rath, Amitav and Sherry Lealess (eds), *Technology for People: Forum on South–South Cooperation in Science and Technology (FOSAT)*, Ottawa: Policy Research International Inc.

Ravines, Roger (ed.) (1978), *Tecnología Andina*, Lima: Instituto de Estudios Peruanos.

Reddy, Amulya Kumar (1978), 'An alternative pattern of Indian industrialization', *Human Futures*, **1**, 105–11.

Roche, Marcel (1976), 'Early history of science in Spanish America', *Science*, **194**, 806–10.

Rosenberg, Nathan (1982), *Inside the Black Box: Technology and Economics*, Cambridge: Cambridge University Press.

Rosenberg, Nathan, Ralph Landau and David Mowery (1992), *Technology and the Wealth of Nations*, Stanford, CA: Stanford University Press.

Roy, Ramashray (1984), *Self and Society: A Study in Gandhian Thought*, Tokyo: United Nations University.

Russell, Alan (1999), 'Biotechnology as a technological paradigm in the global knowledge structure', *Technology Analysis & Strategic Management*, **11** (2), 235–54.

Sabáto, Jorge (1972), 'Empresas y Fábricas de Tecnología', Washington, DC, Department of Scientific Affairs, Organization of American States.

Sachs, Ignacy (1971) 'A welfare state in poor countries', *Economic and Political Weekly* (Bombay), **6** (3–4), January, 367–70.

Sachs, Ignacy (1987), *Development and Planning*, Cambridge: Cambridge University Press.

Sachs, Ignacy (1992), 'Transition strategies for the 21st century', *Nature and Resources*, **28** (1), 4–17.

Sachs, Ignacy, D. Thery and K. Vinaver (1974), *Technologies Appropriées pour le Tiers Monde: Vers une Gestion du Pluralisme Technologique*, Paris: Centre International de Recherche sur l'Environment et le Developpement.

Saffo, Paul (2002), 'Untangling the future', *Business 2.0*, 17 May.

Sagasti, Francisco (1972a), 'A systems approach to science and technology policy-making and planning', Studies on Scientific and Technological Development No. 7, Washington, DC: Department of Scientific Affairs, Organization of American States.

Sagasti, Francisco (1972b), 'Towards a new approach for scientific and technological planning', *Social Science Information*, **12** (2), 67–95.

Sagasti, Francisco (1973), 'Underdevelopment, science and technology: the point of view of the underdeveloped countries', in E. Rabinowitch and V. Rabinowitch (eds), *Views of Science, Technology and Development*, Oxford: Pergamon Press, pp. 41–53; published also in *Science Studies*, **3** (1), 47–59.

Sagasti, Francisco (1976a), 'Algunas Ideas para una Estrategia de Desarrollo Científico y Tecnológico', *Cuadernos del Consejo Nacional de la Universidad Peruana*, Nos 22–23.

Sagasti, Francisco (1976b), 'Technological self-reliance and cooperation among third world countries', *World Development*, **4** (10–11), 939–46.

Sagasti, Francisco (1977a), 'Reflexiones sobre la Endogenización de la Revolución Científico-Tecnológica en Países Subdesarrollados', *Interciencia*, **2** (4), 216–21.

Sagasti, Francisco (1977b), *Tecnología, Planificación y Desarrollo Autónomo*, Lima: Instituto de Estudios Peruanos.

Sagasti, Francisco (1977c), 'Remarks on the transition towards a new international scientific and technological order', in *Proceedings of the 8th International Conference of the International Cooperation Institute on 'Scientific and Technological Innovation: Self-Reliance and Co-Operation'*, Ottawa: University of Ottawa Press, pp. 40–49.

Sagasti, Francisco (1977d), 'Guidelines for technology policies', *Science and Public Policy*, **4** (1), 2–15.

Sagasti, Francisco (1978a), 'Hacia un Desarrollo Científico y Tecnológico Endógeno para América Latina', *Comercio Exterior*, **28** (12), 1498–504.

Sagasti, Francisco (1978b), *Science and Technology for Development: Main Comparative Report of the Science and Technology Policy Instruments Project*, Ottawa: International Development Research Centre (also published in French and Spanish).

Sagasti, Francisco (1978c), 'Esbozo Histórico de la Ciencia y Tecnología en América Latina', *Interciencia*, **3** (6), 351–9.

Sagasti, Francisco (1979a), 'Towards endogenous science and technology for another development', *Development Dialogue*, (1), 13–23.

Sagasti, Francisco (1979b), *Technology, Planning, and Self-Reliant Development: A Latin America View*, New York: Praeger.

Sagasti, Francisco (1979c), 'Financing the development of science and technology in the third world', *IFDA Dossier*, (8), 1–12.

Sagasti, Francisco (1979d), 'National science and technological policies for development: a comparative analysis', in J. Ramesh and C. Weiss, jr (eds) (1979), *Mobilizing Technology for World Development*, New York: Praeger, pp. 163–71.

Sagasti, Francisco (1980a), 'The two civilizations and the process of development', *Prospects*, **X** (2), 123–39

Sagasti, Francisco (1980b), 'A review of schools of thought on science, technology, development and technical change', Ottawa: International Development Research Centre.

Sagasti, Francisco (1980c), 'Towards endogenous science and technology for another development', *Technological Forecasting and Social Change*, (16), 321–30; also published in Dieter Ernst (ed.), *The New International Division of Labor, Technology and Underdevelopment Consequences for the Third World*, Frankfurt: Campus Verlag, pp. 592–606.

Sagasti, Francisco (1981), 'Integration of technology transfers with the technical and cultural heritages of the developing countries', in *Technology and Democracy: Impacts of Technological Change on European Society and Civilization,* proceedings of the Fifth Parliamentary and Scientific Conference held in Helsinki, 3–5 June, Strasbourg, Council of Europe.

Sagasti, Francisco (1983a), 'Techno-economic intelligence for development', *IFDA, Dossier,* (35), 17–25.

Sagasti, Francisco (1983b), 'Hacia una Incorporación de la Ciencia y la Tecnología en la Concepción del Desarrollo', *El Trimestre Económico,* L(3) (199), 1627–54.

Sagasti, Francisco (1984), 'Reflections on the United Nations Conference on Science and Technology for Development', in W. Morehouse (ed.), *Third World Panacea or Global Boondoggle? The Conference on Science and Technology for Development Revisited,* Lund: Research Policy Institute, University of Lund, pp. 18–40.

Sagasti, Francisco (1986), 'The technological transformation of China and its social impact: an agenda for policy research', *Interciencia,* 11 (1), 36–9.

Sagasti, Francisco (1988a), 'Crisis y Desafío: Ciencia y Tecnología en el Futuro de América Latina', *Comercio Exterior,* **38** (12), 1107–10.

Sagasti, Francisco (1988b), 'Reinterpreting the concept of development from a science and technology perspective' in E. Baark and U. Svedin (eds), *Man, Nature and Technology: Essays on the Role of Ideological Perceptions,* London: Macmillan Press.

Sagasti, Francisco (1988c), 'Market structure and technological behavior in developing countries', in A. Wad (ed.), *Science, Technology and Development,* Boulder, CO: Westview Press, pp. 149–68.

Sagasti, Francisco (1988d), 'National development planning in turbulent times: new approaches and criteria for institutional design', *World Development,* **16** (4), 431–48.

Sagasti, Francisco (1989a), 'Crisis and challenge: science and technology in the future of Latin America', *Futures,* **21** (2), 161–8.

Sagasti, Francisco (1989b), 'International cooperation in a fractured global order', *Impact of Science on Society,* **39** (155), 207–11.

Sagasti, Francisco (1989c), 'Science and technology policy research for development: an overview and some priorities from a Latin American perspective', *Bulletin of Science, Technology and Society,* **9** (1), 50–60.

Sagasti, Francisco (1989d), 'Vulnerabilidad y Crisis: Ciencia y Tecnología en el Perú de los Ochenta', *Interciencia,* **14** (1), 18–27.

Sagasti, Francisco (1991), 'National strategic planning in a fractured global order', *Development: Journal of the Society for International Development,* (3/4), 11–15.

Sagasti, Francisco (1995), 'Knowledge and development in a fractured global order,' *Futures,* **27** (6), 591–610.

Sagasti, Francisco (1996), 'Strategic planning and management for development in a fractured global order', in J. Rosenhead and A. Tripathy (eds), *Operational Research for Development,* New Delhi: New Age International, pp. 34–61.

Sagasti, Francisco (1997a), 'The twilight of the Baconian age', working paper, Lima, Foro Nacional/Internacional.

Sagasti, Francisco (1997b), 'Development, knowledge and the Baconian age', *World Development,* **25** (10), 1561–8.

Sagasti, Francisco (1999), *The Future of Development Cooperation: Gradual Evolution or Radical Break?* Seventh Annual Hopper Lecture, Ontario: University of Guelph.

Sagasti, Francisco (2000), 'The twilight of the Baconian age and the future of humanity', *Futures*, **32**, 595–602.

Sagasti, Francisco (ed.) (2001), *Development Strategies for the 21st Century: The Case of Peru*, Lima: PERU/Report–Agenda: PERÚ.

Sagasti, Francisco and Gonzalo Alcalde (1999), *Development Cooperation in a Fractured Global Order: An Arduous Transition*, Ottawa: International Development Research Centre.

Sagasti, Francisco and Alberto Aráoz (1975), 'Analysis of the instruments and mechanisms of science and technology policy in developing countries with particular reference to the industrial sector: methodological guidelines for the STPI project', Paris, OECD Development Centre.

Sagasti, Francisco, with the collaboration of Rubén Berríos, Carlos E. Paredes and Gonzalo Garland (1987), 'Market structure and technological behaviour: a study of the edible oils industry in Peru', Geneva: International Labour Office.

Sagasti, Francisco and Keith Bezanson (2001), *Financing and Providing Global Public Goods: Expectations and Prospects*, Stockholm: Ministry for Foreign Affairs of Sweden.

Sagasti, Francisco and Michael E. Colby (1993), 'Eco-development and perspectives on global change from developing countries', in N. Choucri (ed.), *Global Accord: Environmental Challenges and International Responses,* Cambridge, MA: MIT Press, pp. 175–203.

Sagasti, Francisco and Cecilia Cook (1985), 'Tiempos Difíciles: Ciencia y Tecnología en América Latina en el Decenio del los Ochenta', Lima: GRADE.

Sagasti, Francisco and Gonzalo Garland (1985), 'Crisis, knowledge and development: a review of long-term perspectives on science and technology for development', Lima, GRADE.

Sagasti, Francisco and Mauricio Guerrero (1974), *El Desarrollo Científico y Tecnológico en América Latina*, Buenos Aires: BID/INTAL.

Sagasti, Francisco and Max Hernández (1996), 'Agenda: PERÚ and the prospects for democratic governance', *Development, Journal of the Society for International Development*, (3), 30–35.

Sagasti, Francisco and Fernando Prada (2000), 'A science and technology capacity index', Working paper, Lima: FORO, Nacional/Internacional–Agenda: PERÚ.

Sagasti, Francisco, G. Oldham, P. Vorauri and P. Thiongane (1983), *Evaluation of International Foundation for Science (1974–1981)*, Stockholm: International Foundation for Science.

Sagasti, Francisco (1979), *A Review of Schools of Thought on Science, Technology Development and Technical Change*, Ottawa: International Development Research Center.

Salam, Abdus (1991a), *Science, Technology and Science Education in the Development of the South*, Trieste: Third World Academy of Sciences.

Salam, Abdus (1991b), 'Spreading the word', *Nature*, 3 October, p. 437.

Salomon, Jean-Jacques, Francisco Sagasti and Celine Sachs-Jeantet (eds) (1994), *The Uncertain Quest: Science, Technology and Development*, Tokyo: United Nations University Press (also published in French and in Spanish).

Sardar, Ziauddin (1977), *Science, Technology and Development in the Muslim World*, London: Croom Helm.

Sarewitz, Daniel (2000), 'Science policy present: where is the frontier?', Gordon Research Conference on New Frontiers in Science and Technology Policy, 20–25 August, Plymouth, New Hampshire, Center for Science, Policy and Outcomes.

Schot, Johan (2001), 'Towards new forms of participatory technological development', *Technological Analysis & Strategic Management*, **13** (1), 39–52.

Schumacher, E.F. (1973), *Small is Beautiful: Economics as if People Mattered*, New York: Harper and Row.

Schwartz, Eugene S. (1971), *Overskill: The Decline of Technology in Modern Civilization*, Chicago: Quadrangle Books.

Sen, S.N. (1970), 'The introduction of Western science in India during the 18th and the 19th century', in S. Shina (ed.), *Science, Technology and Culture*, New Delhi: India International Center.

Shin, Taeyoung, Soon-Ki Hoong and Hariolf Grupp (1999), 'Technology foresight in Korea and in countries closing the technology gap', *Technological Forecasting and Social Change*, **60**, 71–84.

Shrum, Wesley and Yehouda Shenhav (1995), 'Science and technology in less developed countries', in S. Vasanoff, G.E. Markle, J.C. Peterson and T. Pinch (eds), *Handbook of Science and Technology Studies*, Thousand Oaks, CA: Sage, pp. 633–51.

Singer, Charles (1958), *From Magic to Science*, New York: Dover.

Sirimanne, Shamika (2000), 'Information technology revolution: what about the developing countries', *Information Technology in Developing Countries*, **10** (2), 5–8.

Siu, R.G.H. (1957), *The Tao of Science*, Cambridge, MA: MIT Press.

Snow, C.P. (1963), *The Two Cultures: and a Second Look*, New York: New American Library.

Snyder, Paul (1978), *Towards One Science: the Convergence of Traditions*, London: St Martin's Press.

Stewart, Frances (1978), 'Inequality, technology and payment systems', *World Development*, **6** (3), 275–93.

Stremlau, John (1985), 'Report on the creation of the Pocantico Institute', New York: Rockefeller Brothers Fund.

Sunkel, Osvaldo (1977), 'El Desarrollo de la Teoría del Desarrollo', *Estudios Internacionales*, **10** (40), 33–46.

Sutz, Judith (2000), 'The university–industry–government relations in Latin America', *Research Policy*, **29**, 279–90.

Teubal, Morris, Dominique Foray, Moshe Justman and Ehud Zuscovithch (1996), *Technological Infrastructure Policy: An International Perspective*, Dordrecht: Kluwer Academic Publishers.

Technology Review (2003), '10 Emerging Technologies', *Technology Review*, February.

Thompson, William Irvin (1978), *Darkness and Scattered Light*, New York: Anchor Press, Doubleday.

Tuldar, Rob van and Gerd Junne (1988), *European Multinationals in Core Technologies*, London: John Wiley.

United Nations (various years), *United Nations Statistical Yearbook*, New York: United Nations.

United Nations Advisory Committee on Science and Technology for Development (1989), 'Science, technology and development: the imperative of social innovation', New York: United Nations.

United Nations Conference on Science and Technology for Development (1979), *The Vienna Programme of Action on Science and Technology for Development*, New York: United Nations.

United Nations Development Programme (UNDP) (2000), *Technology for People: A Report on South–South Cooperation in Science and Technology (FOSAT)*, Seoul: UNDP, 14–17 February.

United Nations Development Programme (UNDP) (2001), *Human Development Report 2001: Making New Technologies Work for Human Development*, New York: Oxford University Press.

United Nations Education, Science and Culture Organization (UNESCO) (various years), *World Science Report*, Paris: UNESCO.

United Nations Education, Science and Culture Organization (UNESCO) (various years), *Statistical Yearbook*, Paris: UNESCO.

United Nations Industrial Development Organization (UNIDO) (2002), *Industrial Development Report 2002/2003: Competing Through Innovation and Learning*, Vienna: UNIDO.

United Nations Trade and Development Conference (UNCTAD) (various years), *World Investment Report*, Geneva: UNCTAD.

United States Government (1994), *The President's Official Science and Technology Policy*, Washington DC, United States Government Public Document

Usui, Mikoto (2001), 'Science and technology for poverty alleviation: is it a hubris?', Workshop on Co-Evolution of Technology Impacting Industry and Society, 3 February, Tokyo, Shukutoku University and United Nations University Institute of Advanced Studies.

Vessuri, Hebe (1993), 'The institutionalization process,' in J.J. Salomon, F. Sagasti and C. Sachs-Jeantet (eds), *The Uncertain Quest: Science, Technology and Development*, Tokyo: United Nations University Press.

Wagner, Caroline S., Irene Brahmakulam, Brian Jackson, Anny Wong and Tatsuro Yoda (2001), 'Science and technology collaboration: building capacity in developing countries?', Washington, DC, World Bank/RAND Corporation.

Warren, Michael (1991), 'Using indigenous knowledge in agricultural development', Washington, DC, World Bank Discussion Paper No. 127.

Weinberg, Gregorio (s.f.), 'Consideraciones sobre la Historia de la Tradición Científica del Desarrollo de la Conciencia Social y su Importancia en la Formación de la Conciencia Nacional y Latinoamericana', Buenos Aires: mimeo.

Wernick, Iddo K., Robert Herman, Shekhar Govind and Jesse H. Ausubel (1996), 'Materialization and dematerialization: measures and trends', *Daedalus*, **125** (3), 171–98.

Wertheim, W.F. (1974), *Evolution and Revolution: The Rising Waves of Emancipation*, Harmondsworth: Penguin Books.

Winner, Langdon (1977), *Autonomous Technology*, Cambridge, MA: MIT Press.

World Bank (1998), *World Development Report 1999: Knowledge and Information for Development*, Washington, DC: World Bank.

World Bank (2000), 'The networking revolution opportunities and challenges for developing countries', Washington, DC, World Bank InfoDev Working Paper Series, Global Information and Communication Technologies Department.

World Bank (various years), *World Development Indicators 2001* (in CD-ROM format).

Zey, Michael G. (1994), *Seizing the Future: How the Coming Revolution in Science, Technology, and Industry Will Expand the Frontiers of Human Potential and Reshape the Planet*, New York: Simon and Schuster.

Zuk, Marlene (2001), 'Beyond the science wars: the missing discourse about science and society', *Endeavour*, **25** (1), 44.

Index

Titles of publications are shown in *italics*.

private sector and scientific research 34
problem-oriented programs 105, 106–7,
   112, 114
production systems
  costs 42
  distribution 44–9
  evolution of 19–26
  global linkages 94
  restructuring 43–53
Prometheus 30

quantum mechanics 14
quantum nucleonics 40

RAND index of science and technology
  capacity 71, 120–22, 124–5
relativity theory 13–14
religion, challenge to science 33

science, dissemination 1–8
science push phase 80
science and technology capacity,
  developing countries 58–73
Science and Technology Capacity Index
  63–73, 79, 120–27
  and policy instruments 97–9
Science and Technology for Development, UN Conference on
  (UNCSTD) 102, 104, 105
science and technology policy
  developing countries 78–114
  implementation phase 81
  instruments 93–9
science wars debate 32
scientific publications, inequalities 61
scientific research
  global linkages 94
  20th century 33–6
  and war 27
  see also innovation
service activities, evolution of 19–24
Snow, C.P. 32
social environment for science and
  technology promotion 96
Social Function of Science, The 79
speculative thought 7
  evolution of 11–15, 24–6
statistical analysis of massive data 39
strategy in development 84–8

supply-side policy instruments 91–2
systemic nature of technological
  innovation 36–43
systems approach to science and
  technology policies 80–81

technical cooperation between developing countries (TCDC) 108–9
techno-economic paradigms 49–53
Technological Achievement Index
  120–22, 123
technological base 7
  evolution of 15–19, 24–6
technological innovation, systemic
  nature 36–43
technology-intensive goods, exports 47
technology sources, global linkages 94
technology transfer and systems analysis
  phase 80
telephones, unequal access 61
Teubal, M. 88, 91
Trade-Related Aspects of Intellectual
  Property Rights (TRIPS) 48
traditional knowledge, developing
  countries 54–5
triple crisis 24–6
*Two Cultures and the Scientific Revolu-
  tion, The* 32

UN Advisory Committee on Science and
  Technology for Development
  (ACSTD) 129–32
UN Conference on Science and Technol-
  ogy for Development (UNCSTD)
  102, 104, 105
UN Financing System for Science and
  Technology for Development
  (UNFSSTD) 105
UNESCO index of science and technol-
  ogy capacity 72, 120–22, 126–7

war, and scientific research 27
Washington Consensus 82
Wertheim, W.F. 9
Western dominance of science 1–2, 3–4,
  10–11
World Plan of Action on Science and
  Technology for Development 104
World War II, scientific research 27